# Dominance and Dependency

# Dominance and Dependency

## Liberalism and National Policies in the North Atlantic Triangle

John Hutcheson



McCLELLAND AND STEWART

*The Canadian Publishers*
McClelland and Stewart Limited
25 Hollinger Road
Toronto, Ontario

CANADIAN CATALOGUING IN PUBLICATION DATA

Hutcheson, John, 1940-
Dominance and dependency

Bibliography: p.
ISBN 0-7710-4301-5

1. Canada – Relations (general) with the United States. 2. United States – Relations (general) with Canada. 3. Canada – Economic policy. 4. Canada – Social conditions. I. Title.

FC249.H88 301.29'71'073 C77-001747-9
F1029.5.U6H88

Printed and Bound in Canada

# Contents

# Acknowledgements

I wish to thank the students in my social science courses at York University who have given me a chance to work out some of the themes of this book. Also I wish to thank the members of St. Patrick's College, Carleton University, for their hospitality while I was completing the writing of the book.

# Introduction

It can be said that Canadian society is marked by three basic contradictions. There is the bi-national nature of the country, the division between French-speaking Canada and English-speaking Canada. There is the contradiction between the regions, with their provincial governments, and the Confederation with its central government. And there is the fundamental problem which results from the relationship between Canada and the United States. (This point has been made by Abraham Rotstein in *The Precarious Homestead,* p. 5. And it has been discussed at length in Herschel Hardin's important study, *A Nation Unaware.*)*

This book is concerned principally with the third contradiction, that which arises from Canada's relationship with the United States. It is a limited study of Canada's economic and social history and does not purport to suggest that the other contradictions are less important. In fact Canada's international economic history cannot be discussed without reference to domestic concerns since the nature of Canada's relationship with other countries is not only the result of the policies of the significant foreign societies, but also grows out of the nature of Canadian society.

This book is not a textbook in the sense of a book that attempts to deal adequately with all the major events or facts of concern to a society. It is by no means an account of all the social forces that have been important in our past or our present. It will be obvious that I have based my work on published sources and I cannot claim originality by the presentation of hitherto unknown facts. Thus what I have attempted to do is to produce a book which is both a synthesis of some of the existing literature and an interpretation of Canadian society which can provide a framework for more detailed study.

I hope the book will be of use to students of the social sciences and history as well as to those studying Canadian society. Implicit in the method I have used is an appeal to social scientists to study society historically and equally an appeal to historians to study history with reference to the social sciences. For those who wish to categorize I should say that it was my intention to make a contribution to the study of "the history of society." (Compare E.J. Hobsbawm, "From Social History to the History of Society.")

In writing on the themes I have chosen one inevitably runs the risk of being accused of special pleading and bias. Obviously my interpretation is selective, as is all analysis. The challenge is to be selective without thereby distorting the analysis and ignoring relevant facts. I hope that I have managed to do this. It seems to me that the subject is sufficiently important that it should be made the object of academic enquiry, and there are still grounds for disagreement with existing interpretations.

It has been apparent for at least a decade now that there is need for concern about the extent to which we, as a society, "know ourselves." For example, a very wide range of intellectual opinion in the 1960's was reflected in a collection of essays edited by Al Purdy under the title, *The New Romans.* In that collection the strong nationalism of Farley Mowat and Laurier Lapierre was modified by the ambiguities of William Kilbourn, Larry Zolf, and Desmond Pacey, and violently opposed by the pro-Americanism of Robert Fulford and Irving Layton. When reading such a collection it soon becomes obvious that these writers have very different conceptions of the past and present nature of Canadian society. In particular they are likely to have very different views of what are the central problems in Canadian society.

It seems probable that in many cases differences in opinions about contemporary problems are related to different interpretations of the past. And each interpretation of the past is likely to lead to a different assessment of the significance of any particular problem. The purpose of this study is to suggest an interpretation of Canadian society that focuses on Canada's economic development within the international context of the North Atlantic triangle. The obvious conclusion of such an approach is that our relationship with the United States has become increasingly important. It is also my conclusion that this relationship is a problem in our national life. There are economic difficulties that result from the relationship that are of such magnitude as to call into question the very survival of Canada as a nation. My standpoint is nationalist, as opposed to continentalist, in the sense that I hold the view that we live in a unique society with its own culture and values and that our national survival is desirable.

A theme that is sometimes explicit in this study, and sometimes implicit, is that the circumstances of Canadian society have produced a link between liberalism and continentalism. This creates a major problem for Canadian nationalists because liberalism is a dominant ideology and is strongly associated with values which are important to most Canadians. It is evident, however, that liberalism has not solved many of the problems of social development. In the scale of the whole of humanity Canada is by and large a prosperous country and her problems may seem small, but few would deny that there are difficulties confronting us and they are important for those of us who live here.

Critics are often themselves criticized for having no alternative. They may be accused of creating a feeling of pessimism based on a deterministic view of history. The point of social criticism is not simply to assess blame for the past, but rather to indicate the process by which events have given rise to the present situation. At many points in our past an alternative policy was a possibility. Thus there is implicit an alternative present and certainly, what is of greater importance, an alternative future.

*Complete details of publication are cited in the Bibliography, below.

# ONE
# Interpretations of Canadian Society

In the nineteenth century Canada's relationship with the United States was the subject of the national policy. But following World War I the national policy was concerned more with public welfare and federal-provincial relations. In the 1960's it appeared that the issue of American influence in Canada would become a major concern but it was generally overshadowed by the pressing concern with the subject of bilingualism and biculturalism.

What this has meant then is that, for much of the twentieth century, the national policy has failed to reflect one of the essential features of Canadian society. Just as Canadian policy has often failed to respond to the requirements of Canadian society, so have historians and social scientists often missed essential points in their interpretation of our life as a nation. Some schools of thought have been misleading and in recent years especially they have crowded out the original and fruitful theories that had begun to develop.

A major thesis of this study is that both policies and interpretations of Canada can be divided into two basic and opposing categories. They are either nationalist or they are continentalist. The distinction is not always overt or conscious, in the case of both policies and interpretations. A policy which is intended to be nationalist may in fact have continentalist ramifications because of unforeseen circumstances. An interpretation of Canadian society may be continentalist because the theorist is employing concepts which lead his thought in that direction.

Continentalism has always been fairly clearcut. Continentalists see Canada as an extension of the United States, with the essential distinction lying in the political boundary. Geographically, economically, culturally, and perhaps ultimately politically, Canada is part of a North America defined by the United States. Some continentalists regard this as both inevitable and desirable, some regard it as merely inevitable. Broadly speaking, the nationalist position is that Canada is a unique society with its own culture and values and its survival is desirable though not necessarily certain. The nationalist position, however, has been complicated by Canada's location in the North Atlantic triangle.

Confederation was clearly a nationalist measure. Yet the Fathers of Confederation saw Canada as part of the British Empire. In fact the nationalism of many nineteenth-century Canadians explicitly invoked a scheme of imperial confederation in which Canada would play a dominant role. (See Carl Berger, *The Sense of Power.* Also Berger's article, "The True North Strong and Free".)

Stephen Leacock, for example, said he was an Imperialist "because I will not be a Colonial" (quoted in Berger, *Sense of Power,* p. 259). The imperial nationalists saw that a major problem for Canada was protection from the United States. Eventually of course their solution, whatever one might think of its merits, was rendered unworkable by the collapse of the British imperial system.

In the early years of this century a growing sense of nationhood was reflected in political events, such as the 1911 election which the Conservatives won on the platform of "No Truck nor Trade with the Yankees," and cultural developments as witnessed by the power and forcefulness of the artists who were to become known as the Group of Seven. Then the participation of Canada in World War I was seen as an example of Canada's new role in the world. In 1919 A.Y. Jackson wrote: "We are no longer humble colonials, we've made armies, we can also make artists, historians and poets" (*Rebel, IV,* November 1919, quoted in R. Craig Brown and Ramsay Cook, *Canada: 1896–1921*, p. 305). Following the war the feeling of confidence in the future was recorded at the University of Toronto in a building erected by the Massey family to the memory of Hart Massey. The frieze around the dining room at Hart House is a quotation from John Milton's *Areopagitica:*

Methinks I see in my mind a noble and puissant nation, rousing herself like a strong man after sleep, and shaking her invincible locks. Methinks I see her as an eagle mewing her mighty youth, and kindling her undazzled eyes at the full midday beam. ...

The war also had an effect on Canadian scholarship as can be seen from the outstanding example of Harold Innis. According to Donald Creighton, Innis had been convinced that, through the war, Canada had become a mature country. It was the need to explain Canada, and to help Canadians understand themselves, that directed Innis' approach to a new interpretation of Canadian society. (See Donald Creighton, *Harold Adam Innis,* p. 56.)

Innis was not the only historian whose work reflected the new situation. But the situation was complicated. The 1920's saw a period of confused nationalism and the development of strongly anti-nationalist attitudes. (These changes are discussed by Donald Creighton in his 1956 essay "Towards the Discovery of Canada." See also Ramsay Cook, "La Survivance: English-Canadian Style.") While the decline of the British Empire certainly was removing one of the complexities of Canadian life, the process of decline was only slowly perceived and Canada's changing relationship to the United States was often obscured by the shadow of Britain. In 1926 the refusal of Governor General Lord Byng to grant Mackenzie King a dissolution of parliament was considered by many Canadians to be an act of imperial arrogance suggesting that Canada had not yet progressed beyond the 1830's. King's response was a "political nationalism" directed against imperial interference. In the next election, King's "political nationalism" was more popular than Meighen's "economic nationalism." (See W.L. Morton, *The Progressive Party in Canada,* p. 261.)

After the Great War Canadians no longer asked what kind of British society was to be created, but rather what kind of Canadian society lay in the future. Some interpreted this as a progress from colony to nation even to the extent of seeing an alliance with the United States as Canadian nationalism in defiance of the old colonial loyalism. This was not entirely beside the point, since there were Canadians for whom patriotism was directed toward the Empire and not just toward Canada. This type of nationalism, however, neglected the fact that the United States was becoming a major international power and in particular a dominant factor in the Canadian economy.

The interpretation of the events of these years has been well described by Professor Donald Creighton. The early nationalist Canadian historians (G.M. Wrong, Chester Martin, and R.G. Trotter) "saw that the achievement of Canadian nationality was a dual, not a single process. They did not make the mistake of identifying national autonomy simply and exclusively with emancipation from British control; and they realized that the maintenance of a separate political existence in a continent dominated by the United States was a more important and more difficult achievement." (*Towards the Discovery of Canada,* p. 51)

By the 1930's, however, the continental approach to Canadian history had become fashionable. This obviously had profound implications for the assessment of Canada's relationship to the United States. The continentalists took the view that the struggle for autonomy within the British Empire had been the sole interest of Canadians. The question of an independent political identity within North America appeared to them to be of minor concern.

The popularity of continentalist views in the 1930's did not mean the complete triumph of their assumptions. Innis and Creighton, for example, were writing in that decade and one of the products of the historical thought of the 1930's was John Bartlet Brebner's *North Atlantic Triangle.* Brebner showed that the history of Canada could only be understood by reference to shifts in the power relationships along all three sides of the North Atlantic triangle formed by the United States, the United Kingdom, and Canada. Brebner did not, however, entirely escape from the continentalist view of Canada, a development not unrelated perhaps to the fact that he had taken up residence at Columbia University in New York. He was even sufficiently myopic to refer to the United States and Canada as "the Siamese twins of N. America who cannot separate and live" (Preface to the original edition).

It is only to be expected that the 1930's should have witnessed a critical point in the writing of Canadian history. For by the 1930's it was apparent that the old national policy had collapsed and Canada had entered a new imperial relationship with the States. Some nationalist historians, such as Creighton, opted for a fatalistic approach which mourned the failure of the National Policy and which glorified the past. This tradition was to end in 1965 with George Grant's *Lament for a Nation.* The majority of the historians however, became continentalists, and opposed nationalist statements as outmoded at best and likely to subvert the wellbeing of society.

It was not until after the appearance of George Grant's book that it became apparent that there was also a strong current of nationalism in Canada which often defined itself by reference to the United States and which did not regard the disappearance of Canada as inevitable. Thus since the 1930's Canadians have been confronted with a variety of interpretations of the nature of Canadian society and also have been involved in a political debate about the kind of policies that are appropriate to the circumstances. While continentalist interpretations and policies have been dominant, they have been challenged by an alternative tradition.

*New Societies*

One of the issues implicit in the distinction between continentalists and nationalists is the interpretation of the origins of Canadian society. If Canada's origins were substantially the same as those of the United States so that Canada was virtually an extension of her neighbour, then the continentalist view of Canadian society would be considerably strengthened. If, however, the roots of Canadian society were markedly distinct from those of the United States, it would be misleading to analyse Canada by reference to American parameters.

Of course there are many points of similarity between the origins of the two societies and these similarities have encouraged many Canadian social scientists to interpret their world according to patterns developed in the United States. This tendency was reinforced by the fact that U.S. academic prestige was exceptionally high for many years and models of society that were developed in the United States in the 1950's had considerable impact on historians and social scientists everywhere. This is not merely of academic interest because the claim was being made that American society provided a model for the rest of the world. By emulating the United States other countries could be freed from internal strife and the fear of revolutionary upheavals. In Canada in particular the impact of American models of society had very widespread ramifications.

U.S. academics portrayed their country as the model for development. It was the "First New Nation." Consider, for example, the following passage from a much lauded book by a professor of history at Harvard University:

> What was essentially involved in the American Revolution was not the disruption of society, with all the fear, despair, and hatred that that entails, but the realisation, the comprehension and fulfillment, of the inheritance of liberty and of what was taken to be America's destiny in the context of world history. (Bernard Bailyn, *The Ideological Origins of the American Revolution*, p. 19)

What especially was considered to be "new" about the United States was that it was a classless society without political movements based on class interests. In a world that was filled with social conflict there was something attractive in the model of a society apparently characterized by liberty and unanimity.[1]

In the United States the assumptions of uniqueness go back a long way. (This point will be discussed in more detail in chapter 3.) As early as 1783 Hector Saint Jean de Crèvecoeur, who had gone to the United States after the defeat of Montcalm at Quebec, wrote his *Lettres d'un Fermier Américain* which promoted the myth of an American society in which man lived in harmony with nature, a society in which there was a return to Eden to the extent that society could begin anew. It is also true that at least as early as the 1850's, when Melville published his novel *Redburn*, the view was expressed that the American dream might in fact be a nightmare; but this theme has remained a "counter-culture" view in the States, as was still being demonstrated in the late 1960's by the movie *Easy Rider*.

Even in the 1950's it could not be easily maintained that the United States was free from internal strife. Racial discrimination and violence was obvious. Many Americans, moreover, believed that the country was threatened by the internal subversion of a highly developed communist movement and they reacted with ferocity. Yet the image of the United States as the model future society was carefully fostered. One book which had a remarkable success was *The Liberal Tradition in America* by Louis Hartz, a professor at Harvard University. Hartz's book was particularly successful because it managed to explain even the "paranoid style" of American life by reference to the dominance of the liberal tradition. As we shall see later, the theoretical model which Hartz developed was also thought to be useful in accounting for the development of Canadian politics.

In Hartz's view American society was based on unanimity. There was no revolutionary tradition in America because of America's appearance as a "new" nation. In Europe feudal society had given rise to a liberal movement and to liberal political parties. But in America liberalism had appeared, not as a political movement, but as the "American way of life." Thus while American society was permeated by a "nationalist articulation" of the liberalism of John Locke, there is no understanding in America of the fact that these views are historically associated with the political development of the European bourgeoisie. This lack of recognition, Hartz suggests, explains "the odd fact that while the Americans are a kind of national embodiment of the concept of the bourgeoisie, they have rarely used that concept in their social thought" (*The Liberal Tradition in America*, p. 51).[2]

Hartz uses this argument to explain a mood of absolutism in American society, a phenomenon which Toqueville had also attempted to explain:

> a sense of community based on a sense of uniformity is a deceptive thing. It looks individualistic and in part it actually is. It [does] not tolerate internal relationships of disparity. ... But in another sense it is profoundly anti-individualistic, because the common standard is its very essence, and deviations from that standard inspire it with an irrational fright.

As the philosopher Santayana once said, "even what is best in America is compulsory."

The element of Hartz's analysis which has attracted most attention in Canada, however, is the concept that American society was "founded" as a liberal society. It "fragmented" from European society in the seventeenth century, carrying with it only a limited set of the social relations and ideas of that larger society. This explanatory model was further developed by Hartz and others in a collection entitled *The Founding of New Societies.*

The "new societies" are those founded by Europeans in the United States, English and French Canada, Latin America, South Africa, and Australia. These "fragments" of Europe are determined by their "point of departure" from Europe. The settlers represent only a "fragment" of the population of the mother country. French Canada and Latin America are "feudal fragments" because their founders brought "feudal" ideas with them; the United States, English Canada and Dutch South Africa are liberal fragments and Australia is a "radical fragment" in that it was founded by bearers of working-class ideologies of mid-nineteenth century Britain. The ideology of the fragment is frozen at the point of departure from Europe and is no longer in conflict with the other ideologies found in the European setting.

The claim that the United States and Canada originated as liberal societies appeared to be useful in some respects. European liberalism developed as societies characterized by peasants and landlords transformed themselves into industrial societies. This historical dimension was missing in North America and liberalism was originally imported into the colonial commercial society that existed prior to industrialization. Yet the argument was filled with difficulties because of the ambiguities of the concept of "liberal society."

Hartz's own analysis is open to several objections. First he assumes that a "liberal" society is one without real social divisions. Even if it were true that ideologically Americans are a "national embodiment of the concept of the bourgeoisie," this would not mean that there are no real class divisions within the society. It is very hard to understand how a serious historian can argue that American society is one which "does not tolerate internal relationships of disparity." Secondly, and perhaps more important, Hartz's analysis moves almost constantly on the plane of ideology, without much reference to real social relations. According to him, liberalism and socialism are ideological phenomena which are in some uncertain way related to the "feudal ethos." The "feudal ethos" appears in some vague way to be linked to the French pre-revolutionary *ancien régime*, but the connection between ideas and social structures is not very clearly developed.

The usage of the word "liberal" has become imprecise (see chapter 5), and Hartz's concept of "liberal society" is even less satisfactory in its application to Canadian history than it was in his study of the United States.

One of the contributors to *The Founding of New Societies* was a Canadian historian, Kenneth McRae. McRae concluded that

Canada could be analysed as a "liberal fragment" of European society, founded in much the same way as the American colonies that became the United States. New France was not of course, like the American colonies, founded on the "prevailing ethos of religious dissent, individual freedom and limited government." In French Canada one could identify "a theme of theoretical absolutism," but because of the distances involved and France's preoccupation with Europe, "the essence of Canadian feudalism is its mildness, its relaxation, its absence of systematic harshness or oppression." (See Kenneth D. McRae, "The Structure of Canadian History," in L. Hartz, ed., *The Founding of New Societies,* pp. 222 and 224.) MacRae also rejected the view that the Loyalist immigration fundamentally differentiated Canada from the United States, except politically. The maritime Loyalists, he suggests, were a representative cross-section of American seaboard society and the Upper Canadian Loyalists were soon outnumbered by other immigrants. "The Upper Canadian Loyalists became simply a phase of the unrolling of the North American frontier ..." (*ibid.*, p. 236). Thus the tradition of Loyalism should not be allowed to obscure the "important parental relationship" between Canada and the United States (*ibid.*, p. 239).

Hartz's concepts were, however, soon used to draw the opposite conclusion by the Canadian social scientist Gad Horowitz, who wanted to explain not the uniformity but the diversity of political ideas to be found in Canada. (See G. Horowitz, "Conservatism, Liberalism, and Socialism in Canada: An Interpretation." See also Horowitz's review of George Grant's *Lament for a Nation*, "Tories, Socialists and the Demise of Canada.") Horowitz drew the conclusion that what is un-American about English Canada can be summed up in one word: British. The American society was the product of a "liberal" revolution, and it has remained monolithically "liberal" until the present day. English Canada's dominant ideology has always been a liberalism quite similar to the American but there has also been a Britishness about English Canada which has expressed itself in two ideologies each of which is "alien," beyond the pale of legitimacy, in the United States. These two ideologies are "conservatism" and "socialism." Conservatism means public order and tradition as opposed to individualism. English Canada was stamped by the toryism of Loyalists. "Their influence has been crucial and pervasive" – for example in the persistence in Canada of authoritarian values. Also, there has been in Canada (a result of immigration, too, but this time of British immigrants in the late nineteenth century) a strong component of socialism. In fact toryism and socialism have reinforced each other, because unlike liberalism, they share a commitment to the collectivity. Socialists in fact "have a tory conception of society."

Horowitz rejected McRae's analysis and also Hartz's conclusion about the identity of the Canadian fragment, but he did not reject Hartz's analytic framework. Horowitz argues that because Canada has a significant socialist tradition, the tory component of the Canadian past must have been of sufficient importance that Canada should not be described as a liberal fragment.

Horowitz also rejects the notion implied by Seymour Martin Lipset (in *The First New Nation)* that Canada was a "feudal" fragment because of the presence of tory Loyalists. Rather Canada should be described as a liberal fragment with a significant "tory presence" and eventually also a "socialist presence." In fact Horowitz admits that English-speaking Canadian society does not lend itself to Hartz's analysis too readily because it is difficult to "put one's finger on the point of congealment" of the culture. Whereas the United States broke completely from Britain, Canada's ties remained for much longer, and it is even difficult to identify a precise breaking point. Thus some questions remain unclear. If the breaking point is late, then the socialist tradition can be said to come into Canada with immigrants; if it is early, then the socialist tradition is indigenous and grows out of the tory presence.

Horowitz has many interesting things to say about Canadian politics and the cultural differences between Canada and the United States. But his weakness is in explaining Canada's difference from the United States in purely ideological and political terms. Horowitz's argument is not an adequate rejection of the continentalist position. What is "un-American" about English-speaking Canada is *not* that it is "British"; what is "un-American" about English-speaking Canada is that it is *Canadian.*

Economic liberalism has historically been modified in its workings in Canada because the circumstances of Canadian development have necessitated a departure from laissez-faire policies. It was not the survival of tory values, perpetuated by the British connection, that provided the rationale for government enterprise. The differences between Canada and the United States are not merely political ones. The role of the Canadian government, as Innis showed us, was determined by the Canadian context. National policies were necessary for the survival of Canada in the face of the continental expansion of the United States. By understanding Canada from this perspective, Innis could see the whole of Canadian history as "one long period of economic planning."

*Innis and The Staple Approach*

The staple theory emerged against the background of a generally popular "frontier" approach to Canadian history. The frontier approach stressed the agrarian aspects of society and extolled the progressive and democratic aspects of the new society. This approach was continentalist to the extent that it stressed obvious similarities between Canada and the United States. In fact the concepts were heavily influenced by the work of the American historian Frederick Jackson Turner. (See J.M.S. Careless, "Frontierism, Metropolitanism, and Canadian History." Careless refers to the work of Innis and Creighton as the Laurentian School.)

Innis did not by any means neglect the impact of the Canadian environment and geography. In fact he spent considerable time travelling across the country and into the north while preparing himself for his work, and the awareness of geographical factors is fundamental to his work (see Donald Creighton, *Harold Adams Innis,* pp. 58–59). But Innis recognized the equally important point that the "frontier" was only the end of a long chain of commercial links that bound farmers and miners to merchants and bankers. The links extended through the Canadian cities and outside the country to the imperial centres.

The single most important point to result from Innis' work was the conclusion that Canada "emerged not in spite of geography, but because of it." (See *The Fur Trade in Canada,* p. 393.) In other words Canada was not an artificial creation, maintained by the existence of the political division of the forty-ninth parallel or even by the accidents of past patterns of immigration. Canada had been created as a modern nation as a result of its own specific environment.

Innis was not, however, a geographical determinist and his work should not be read in that way. It was the manner in which Canada's geography was exploited that was critical. Traders and settlers had exploited the natural resources in response to social conditions that existed, to some extent in Canada, but, even more significantly, elsewhere. Canadian society had been historically created as traders and settlers developed a series of staple export trades that sent Canadian resources to markets in other countries. Exploration and immigration had been linked to the requirements of export markets.

C.R. Fay, who was teaching at the University of Toronto when Innis arrived there, had already defined the stages of growth in Canada by reference to successive staple exports and had stressed the importance of transportation and commodity specialization between developed and satellite countries. (See R. Neill, *A New Theory of Value: The Canadian Economics of H. A. Innis,* p. 39.)

Canadian development had taken place in the context of an international economy. In fact as Innis showed, this meant in the context of an imperial economic system as Canada had been linked to a series of dominant markets. In his conclusion to *The Fur Trade in Canada,* Innis provided a far-ranging generalization about the nature of Canadian society. His analysis stressed the fact that Canada had been at the "margin" of western civilization, rather than at the centre, and thus Canada's role had been to provide a succession of staple products, raw materials, for the manufacturing industries of the centre countries. Canada had been linked to imperial centres through cod and fur exports, then through forest products, beginning with square timber and progressing to pulp and paper, and also through agriculture and mining.

Each staple product made its own particular contribution to the pattern of development. But it was not only economic development that turned on the staple exports. Government activity was largely directed to the attempt to continue to provide staples to more industrial societies. One of the staple export trades, the fur trade, had even defined Canada's political boundaries. But if staples could make a country, they could also have less favourable effects and the geographical unity of Canada became less secure as the industrialization of the United States gave rise to new demands on Canada. Innis emphasized the long-term consequences of reliance on staple exports: weakness in other lines of development and dependence on industrialized countries for markets and supplies of manufactured goods.

The emphasis is not merely on resources, but on the exploitation of resources. This leads Innis into the exploration of the economic framework within which exploitation was encouraged. He drew particular attention to the way in which capital and transportation routes were organized. This aspect of the staple theory allowed for the connection of what could be called economic history to social and political history, and Innis' work is well complemented by the work of Donald Creighton (see particularly *The Commercial Empire of the St. Lawrence.*)

Innis's historical analysis was of course much more complex than this simple summary, but we can see even from this brief outline that he provided a powerful method of examining some of the fundamental themes in Canadian history. The importance of the staple approach lies in its suggestion that staple exports have been more than just important sectors of the economy. Economic historians have frequently analysed economic growth in terms of "leading sectors" which acted as catalysts for more general economic development throughout the rest of the economy. In the Canadian case, however, the staple export sectors have not merely been agents in economic growth. They have dominated the whole of Canadian society through their economic, social, and political, ramifications. Canadian society has literally grown around the staple activities and has figuratively grown in their image.

This is not to say that the staple approach accounts fully for all aspects of Canadian society. There are important questions which lie outside its purview as there are also some aspects of Canadian economic development which have not been satisfactorily explained in terms of the staple approach. There are limitations in Innis's own work which arise from his preoccupation with the price system and market organization as the mechanism of economic development.

Innis saw economic development occurring as a price system or market organization extended itself geographically, opening up new areas for profitable economic activity. In the case of Canada in particular, the application of established technologies to newly found natural resources provided a major incentive for the extension of European, and later American, market organization. (This is also a main theme of Kari Levitt's study, *Silent Surrender.)* The weakness of this analysis lies in its emphasis on commodity trade and its relative neglect of the organization of commodity production. Industry is seen as an outgrowth of trade and there is insufficient analysis of the social re-organization involved in industrialization. Of course the organization of trade is important, and Innis did show how trade led to new forms of production and social organization. But a greater concern with the social organization of production was needed to make the staple approach fruitful in analysing the range of social relationships that have characterized Canadian society and that have marked its particular type of economic development. In addition, such a modification of the staple approach was needed to explain the international framework better by means of a deeper analysis of imperialism.

Chapters 2 – 5 of this book provide what could be called an extension of the staple approach. In chapter 2 there is an analysis of the imperial policies which provided the framework for the colonization and development of Canada. Sir John A. Macdonald's National Policy was developed in the context of the British imperial system and the decline of the system had far-reaching consequences for the National Policy.

One of the factors in the decline of the British Empire was the growing power of the United States. The way in which the United States rose to world leadership, and some of the consequences, is the subject of chapter 3. In chapters 4 and 5 I have examined the interaction of the changing international situation with Canadian economic policies and political ideals.

## Notes

**1.** This view of the United States was not of course new in the 1950's. It was a commonplace of nineteenth century thought that America was classless, and this opinion was cultivated by the American upper class itself. The American sociologist G. William Domhoff makes this point in an anecdote concerning Marietta Peabody Tree. "a member of the upper class if there ever was one." Mrs. Tree recalls that the "first and only time" her grandmother ever slapped her was when, as a young girl, Marietta referred to an acquaintance as "very middle class." After the slap came these stern grandmotherly words: "There are no classes in America, upper, lower or middle. You are never to use that term again." (See Domhoff, *The Higher Circles,* p. 72.)

**2.** According to Hartz (see *The Liberal Tradition in America,* p. 6), the absence of a feudal tradition in America accounts for the absence of both revolutionary liberalism and socialism: "Socialism is largely an ideological phenomenon (and thus Marx was wrong to attribute it to the objective movement of economic forces) arising out of the principles of class and the revolutionary liberal revolt against them which the old European order inspired. It is not accidental that America which has uniquely lacked a feudal tradition has uniquely lacked also a socialist tradition. The hidden origin of socialist thought everywhere in the West is to be found in the feudal ethos. The *ancien régime* inspires Rousseau; both inspire Marx."

# TWO
# Nineteenth-Century Imperialism and the National Policy

Canada's dependent position has become a subject of much concern in recent years. This is undoubtedly a reflection of the growing recognition that our future is increasingly uncertain. It is no longer possible to assume that this country has successfully made the jump to independence and guaranteed economic development. Every day we are faced with the growing penetration of our society by U.S. investment. We face a troubled economic future and the fundamentally related question of our cultural survival since U.S. investment has brought with it U.S. cultural values.

We should of course avoid the tendency to misinterpret the situation by portraying Canada in terms used to describe the so-called "third world." In fact the term itself is very vague and many related analyses of underdevelopment are of little use in analysing the Canadian situation.

The attempt to specify development or underdevelopment by purely statistical series is misleading. The usual measures when applied to Canada show a contradictory result. Obviously per capita income, the first category usually used, is very high in Canada, in fact among the highest in the world. But what about the profound regional differences within Canada? And in what direction is her per capita income likely to move relative to that of other countries? We should also consider whether Canada will be able to support her already relatively small population under the present scheme of development. This has in fact been a constant concern in

Canadian history, as from 1850 to 1950 immigration was balanced by emigration to the United States. (The figures for 1851 to 1950 are: immigration 7,790,000; emigration 7,260,000. See R.E. Caves and R.H. Holton, *The Canadian Economy,* p. 52.)

It is also common to use the sectoral distribution of the labour force as an index. In 1971, 21.3 per cent of the non-agricultural work force was in manufacturing, a drop from 24.5 per cent in 1965. The figures for the same years for the United States showed a decline from 29.7 per cent to 26.3 per cent. Does this mean that Canada is "more advanced" than her neighbour? Or is Canada underdeveloped because her exports are so overwhelmingly primary products? What is the significance of being the world's highest per capita importer of manufactured goods ($463 per capita in 1969)?

In 1970, 68 per cent of Canada's exports went to the United States and 71 per cent of Canada's imports came from that country. Furthermore, these proportions have been increasing in recent years. Dependence on bilateral trade is usually taken as an index of dependency and economic instability. And what sort of development is it that leads to a situation where two-thirds of manufacturing and of mining and smelting are in the control of foreign corporations, most of them American? What are the consequences for the future?

The significance of these statistics can only be understood by reference to an historical analysis. A static profile will not tell us anything about our prospects. We have to understand our country by reference to past developments and to the forces that are shaping world history.

One of the implications of the staple approach is that economic development must be interpreted through an understanding of the role of economic policy in the context of international market forces. In the case of Canada the economic policy was primarily the National Policy and the international market forces were determined, largely, first by the industrialization of Great Britain and later by that of the United States.

The National Policy has been the subject of a considerable literature, some of which will be discusssed later. In recent years especially, the National Policy has been generally criticized for its failings. Undoubtedly the results of the policy have been far from satisfactory but many of the criticisms appear to be invoked not by a displeasure with the results but by a distaste for the premises of the policy. Economic historians, for example, who start from a set of assumptions concerning the advantages of laissez-faire are likely to find the policy wanting precisely because it was an attempt to modify the effects of market allocation. Just as many liberal historians are unhappy about nationalism, liberal economists are unhappy about national economic policies.

There is likely also to be disagreement over the significance of the resulting pattern of development. Professor John Dales has argued that the National Policy increased population at the expense of the standard of living. (See J.H. Dales, "Some Historical and Theoretical Comments on Canada's National Policies," also "The Cost of Protectionism with High International Mobility of Factors," and "Protection, Immigration and Canadian Nationalism." See also the discussion by Rotstein, *The Precarious Homestead,* p. 29–31.)

Apart from the possibility that Dales' conclusion is wrong, it is striking that Dales can write about labour mobility and population as abstractions. According to his analysis, Canada would be better off with a higher standard of living and fewer people. But *which* people would no longer be here? Surely this point is important in a discussion of economic development. When the Black Death reduced the population of Europe by one-third, the standard of living for the survivors probably rose, but could that be considered economic development? A society is more than a collection of atomistic consumers who are oblivious of everything other than their own individual satisfaction.

Studies of economic development must be concerned with a wider focus than is prescribed by the confines of neoclassical economic theory. It is also reasonable for economists to be concerned with the survival of the community that, after all, supports them.

Furthermore, we cannot deal with the problems of economic development and national policies without taking into account the constraining framework of imperialism. As Innis showed us, Canada has been in the position of a "peripheral" country, dependent on a series of imperial "centre" countries.

### *Imperialism*[1]

A useful starting point for the discussion is provided by the work of two British historians, Gallagher and Robinson. (J. Gallagher and R. Robinson, "The Imperialism of Free Trade.") As they put it (p. 6):

> The basic fact is that British industrialization caused an everextending and intensifying development of overseas regions. Whether they were formally British or not was a secondary consideration. Imperialism ... may be defined as a sufficient political function of [the] process of integrating new regions into [an] expanding economy; its character is largely decided by the various and changing relationships between the political and economic elements of expansion in any particular region and time.

The essential point to recognize is that capitalism has developed by the extension of capitalist control of production to include more and more of the world's economic activity. This has occurred both within countries and across national boundaries. In the western European countries, for example, agriculture and "traditional" manufacturing (textiles, brewing, construction) were all gradually transformed by the growth of capitalism and have become, almost everywhere, industries characterized by capitalist relations of production. Essentially this means that they are carried out within an economic system whereby the labour of a working class is bought and controlled by the owners of capital, that is, the owners of the means of production, for the purpose of profit.

Capitalists have also extended their control into foreign societies in order to extract a profit from the labour of the foreign working population. This external expansion, like the domestic, has been a revolutionary process, carried out on a world-wide scale. There were massive social upheavals as traditional ways were forcibly changed and more upheavals when some people fought back. Frequently the question of land organization became the key issue, and thus the response of peasant populations became critical. (Even in the twentieth century, many wars have been peasant wars. See Eric Wolf, *Peasant Wars of the Twentieth Century.*) Furthermore, this expansion constitutes imperialism when the penetration of other nations has reached a sufficient level that the pattern of development of the society is controlled by foreign capitalists. This control usually involves the influence of governments, but while it is clear that imperialism inevitably means national domination, it is not identical with colonialism. Imperialism may or may not promote colonialism depending on the circumstance in the countries involved. However, imperialism always leads to some form of political and cultural domination and usually to some degree of colonization by representatives of the imperial power.

By identifying imperialism with the extension of capitalist control, it is possible to analyse imperialism as it has developed with capitalism. It is possible to identify *three* chronological phases, associated with phases in the world-wide development of capitalism. These can be called "mercantile imperialism," "free-trade imperialism," and "national imperialism." The three phases can be outlined by a brief historical discussion. In the course of this discussion two further terms will be introduced: "formal empire" and "informal empire."

Let us look first at "mercantile imperialism," also known simply as "mercantilism." The expansion of the European powers, and eventually of European capitalism, began with Spain and Portugal, essentially as a result of attempts to cut out the middleman role of Arab merchants and to find a direct route to the trade and wealth of the east. The Spanish and Portuguese domination of the whole colonial world did not last long – though its presence is felt to this day in some places. In the late sixteenth century the Dutch rebelled against Spanish control of the Netherlands and, having gained their own freedom, the Dutch merchants immediately founded an East Indian Company and began to deprive other people of theirs. In 1600 English merchants founded their own East India Company and began to compete with the Dutch for pre-eminence in colonial trade. The imperialist policy known as mercantilism was developed in the course of these struggles. The nature of the policy was simple and it was well explained by one of the leading merchants of the English East India Company: "Foreign trade produces riches, riches power, power preserves our trade and religion" (Sir Josiah Child, quoted in Peter Gay, *The Enlightenment*, vol. 2, p. 344).

The aim of English policy was revealed by Sir George Downing's remark: "If England were once brought to a navigation as cheap as Holland's, Good Night Amsterdam." The English Navigation Acts of 1651 formalized the main features of mercantilism. The colonies were brought under the control of the government, thus ensuring that economic developments within the colonies were favourable to the interests of the capitalists in the metropolitan country. And trade with the colonies was monopolized by British and colonial shipping, thus excluding foreign capitalists from the exploitation. Naturally the English and the Dutch, along with other European powers, did not restrict their interest to the wealth of the east. They also pursued wealth in the Caribbean and the Atlantic, encroaching on the colonial possessions of Spain and Portugal. (For an economic history of this period see Ralph Davis, *The Rise of the Atlantic Economies.* See also J.H. Parry, *Trade and Dominion,* which discusses the various phases within the mercantilist period.)

Criticisms of these pursuits soon emerged. The anonymous *Tyranipocrit Discovered* published in 1649 was scornful of the motives of English merchants: "Our merchants, they travel by sea and land to make Christian proselytes, chiefly our Indian merchants; but consider their practices, and the profit that we have made by their double dealing, first in robbing of the poor Indians of that which God hath given them, and then in bringing of it home to us, that we thereby may the better set forth and show the pride of our hearts in decking our proud carcasses and feeding our greedy guts with superfluous unnecessary curiosities." (Quoted in Christopher Hill, *The World Turned Upside Down,* pp. 271–72.) But such thoughts were restricted to a minority, and they did little to hamper proceedings.

The struggle between Britain and France for control of the fish and furs of Canada developed within the context of mercantilism. By the time the British had finally won that battle, however, the European and colonial world picture had changed drastically. Spain and Portugal had become backwaters, and by the early nineteenth century the growing independence movements were overthrowing the Spanish hold on large areas of South America. And soon after gaining Canada, the British lost a major portion of their American empire as the American colonists rebelled against the constraints of the imperialist mercantile policy.

In fact the year 1776 was also marked by the appearance of a famous book on economics which suggested that Britain no longer needed the mercantilist regulations. Adam Smith's *Wealth of Nations* contained a full-scale attack on mercantilism and the eighteenth-century colonial system. Smith argued for free trade and liberalism, and these remained the slogans of British capitalists for the next hundred years. Their adoption did not mean an end to imperialism; but simply that a new form of imperialism, "free-trade imperialism," became appropriate to Britain as capitalism produced an industrial revolution and Britain became the "workshop of the world." British economists introduced the arguments for free trade as British industries produced the cheapest manufactured goods which could compete in any market and which *required* growing foreign markets. And in the nineteenth century the British Empire grew with British capitalism and, it should be noted, with liberalism as its ideology. In the words of one historian:

> Whatever his political convictions may have been, the Englishman of the 1870's and 80's was something of a liberal at heart. He believed in freedom, free trade, progress and the Seventh Commandment. ... He was strongly in favour of peace – that is to say, he liked his wars to be fought at a distance and, if possible, in the name of God. (George Dangerfield, *The Strange Death of Liberal England,* p. 7)

Canada played its role in this scheme of things by providing a home for part of the unwanted agricultural population of Britain, by providing a market for British manufactured goods, by providing outlets for profitable capital investment, and at the same time providing cheap primary products which helped make British capitalism more profitable. Canada was of course part of the "formal" empire, though it is significant that it was in this period that Canada was allowed an increasing measure of "Responsible Government." It is, however, necessary to note that only a minority of British emigrants (about 30 per cent from 1812 to 1914) remained within the empire, only one-sixth of British capital exports went to the empire, and in no year in the 1800's did the empire buy more than one-third of Britain's exports.

In other words it is important to recognize that capitalist expansion does not necessarily lead to the creation of formal empire everywhere:

> Whether formal imperialist phenomena show themselves or not is determined not only by the factors of economic expansion but equally by the political and social organizations of the regions brought into the orbit of the expansive society. It is only when the polities of these new regions fail to provide satisfactory condi-

> tions for commercial or strategic integration and when their relative weakness allows, that political power is used imperialistically to adjust those conditions. (Gallagher and Robinson, p. 6)

The strength of British capitalism, backed by the "Pax Britannica," meant that British capitalists could control trade and production in many areas without the establishment of formal colonial political arrangements. In Latin America, for example, Britain replaced Spain as the *de facto* colonial power. (Britain was to be replaced by the United States in a similar manoeuvre in the twentieth century.) The rules of non-formal empire did not, however, exclude "gunboat diplomacy." Palmerston candidly explained the situation in 1860:

> It may be true that trade ought not to be enforced by cannon balls but on the other hand trade cannot flourish without security. It might be said of an European country that trade ought not to be enforced by the cudgels of a police or the sabres and carbines of a gendarmerie, but those cudgels and sabres and carbines are necessary to keep quiet the ill-disposed people whose violence would render trade insecure and thus prevent its operation. (Quoted in W.L. Burn, *The Age of Equipoise,* p. 71)

(On free trade imperialism and non-pacifism see B. Semmell, *The Rise of Free Trade Imperialism.* On the general background of the period see the two important studies by E.J. Hobsbawm, *Industry and Empire* and *The Age of Capital.*)

Neither did "free-trade imperialism" mean the end of controlled colonial trade or of formal empire. It is only necessary to consider the long list of British "acquisitions" even before the colonial "scramble" of the 1880's to see that imperialism still meant direct political subjugation for many people. India, for example, very much part of the formal empire, played a crucial role in the British economic system of the nineteenth century. India supplied raw materials such as hides, oil, dyes, jute, and cotton, all of which were necessary for industrialization in Britain. It also afforded a growing market for English manufactures of iron and cotton, the latter destroying the local textile industry. Trade with India was also the key to trade with China. Of particular value was the export of opium, fostered as a state monopoly by the British government, which in 1870 still accounted for almost half of China's total imports. In addition Britain settled more than one-third of her deficits with Europe and the United States through trade with India, which was perennially in surplus.

Finally, India was a huge reservoir of wealth. It was the taxation of India that enabled British governments to achieve a reputation for economy and financial stability, known as Gladstonian finance, which even now is remembered with nostalgia by conservatives. India paid huge sums, in the form of government charges, for the privilege of being administered by Britain. Leland Jenks summarized the "preposterous" burdens that were imposed on India:

> The costs of the [1857] mutiny, the price of the transfer of the [East India] Company's rights to the Crown, the expenses of simultaneous wars in China and Abyssinia, every governmental item in London that remotely related to India down to the fees of the charwomen in the India Office and the expenses of ships that sailed but did not participate in hostilities and the cost of Indian regiments for six months' training at home before they sailed, – all were charged to the account of the unrepresented ryot. The sultan of Turkey visited London in 1868 in state, and his official ball was arranged for at the India Office and the bill charged to India. A lunatic asylum in Ealing, gifts to members of a Zanzibar mission, the consular and diplomatic establishments of Great Britain in China and in Persia, part of the permanent expenses of the Mediterranean fleet and the entire cost of a line of telegraph from England to India had been charged before 1870 to the Indian Treasury. It is small wonder that the Indian revenues swelled from £33 millions to £52 millions a year during the first thirteen years of Crown administration, and that deficits accumulated from 1866 to 1870 amounting to £11½ millions. (L.H. Jenks, *The Migration of British Capital,* p. 224)

(The role of India is discussed in Lillian Knowles, *Economic Development of the Overseas Empire,* and also in Hobsbawm, *Industry and Empire.* Trade statistics are given by S.B. Saul, *Studies in British Overseas Trade, 1870–1914.*)

In this discussion of nineteenth-century imperialism, Britain has been the focal point. This is appropriate because Britain was obviously the leading imperial power throughout the 1800's. But by the latter part of the century the world of imperialism had changed again. Through the century the French had been developing an empire in North Africa, the Russians an empire in Central Asia, and the United States in North America. These empires had not clashed seriously, though there had been many colonial wars and the imperialist expansion had been marked by bloodshed throughout the world.



But the situation became unstable as a result of developments in the world of capitalism. First, capitalism developed in two countries, Germany and Japan, which did not possess empires, and their economic situation required a forcible rearrangement of the global system controlled by their rivals. And second, confronted by successful competitors, British capitalism was no longer clearly dominant. There thus developed a struggle for markets and raw materials as capitalists from several countries found that they had reached a level of development which both required and permitted imperialist expansion into areas previously dominated by British capitalism. The higher levels of capital sharpened the competition as industrial countries extended their demands for raw materials.

The imperialist rivalries of the late 1800's also led to a new political situation in the capitalist nations themselves, and it is for this reason that I have used the term "national imperialism." First, imperialism provided a basis for a coalition between the industrialists and the nobility in some countries, since the colonies and militarism provided a new role for the nobility. (Joseph Schumpeter, in his essay "Imperialism," attempted to identify imperialism with atavistic forces represented by the feudal nobility. But the new military forces and policies were clearly dictated by the needs of industrial capitalism. Where they were not, as in Russia, the feudal forces did not survive the test of war.)

The imperialist forces claimed that they were defending the nation against foreign enemies and maintaining the strength of the society through their expansionist policies. Their intention was to deflect the increasingly common claim that capitalism was unable to satisfy the needs of the majority and unable to meet the uncertainties associated with the increasingly insistent demands for a more democratic society. Government could no longer be carried on by an executive committee of the propertied classes. A larger number of minor shareholders claimed at least a right to vote for the board of directors.

The advantages of an aggressive imperialist policy were well understood by two spokesmen of the day. First, Cecil Rhodes, a figure who symbolizes the British imperialism of this epoch:

> I was in the East End of London yesterday and attended a meeting of the unemployed. I listened to the wild speeches which were just a cry for "bread," "bread," "bread," and on my way home I pondered over the scene and I became convinced of the importance of imperialism. ...My cherished idea is a solution for the social problem, i.e., in order to save the 40m. inhabitants of the U.K. from a bloody civil war, we colonial statesmen must acquire new lands to settle the surplus population, to provide new markets for the goods produced in the factories and the mines. The Empire, as I have always said, is a bread and butter question. If you want to avoid civil war, you must become imperialist.

In a similar vein, a German industrialist expressed the hope that an imperialist policy could overcome the disturbing signs of class conflict: "We must gain power not only over the legs of the soldiers, but also over their minds and hearts." (Rhodes is quoted in Lenin, *Imperialism: The Highest Stage of Capitalism,* p. 70; the German industrialist in Bukharin, *Imperialism and World Economy.*)

Associated with the new imperialist policies was the deliberate use of racial ideologies to identify the enemy by ethnic or national categories. "Darwinian" interpretations of society were expanded from the individual case to the national level. One of the reasons for the growing popularity of "Darwinian" social theory was the obvious limitation of liberal doctrine in explaining manifest inequality both domestically and internationally. The result of this in the imperialist countries was to redefine nationalist ideologies.

In the early nineteenth century, nationalist movements had had to be democratic and usually republican in opposition to the forces of the "*ancien régime.*" Later in the century, as democracy became a serious threat to the old-style liberalism, liberalism dissociated itself from nationalism. This dissociation created a situation in which nationalist ideologies split according to whether the nations were great powers or subjugated peoples. In the great powers nationalism tended to develop as a form of chauvinism, expressing racial superiority, the right to rule, missionary obligations, etc. Consequently, as a reaction to this, democratic and eventually socialist movements became identified with the struggle for national survival and development in those countries subjected to imperialist domination.[2]

In 1914 the consequences of the new phase of imperial policies became clear. The development of capitalism had led to national war. Wars had in fact become total wars that made clear the relative levels of economic development. The fact that they were national wars also led to the question of what kind of development was desirable and raised even more concern about whose nation was being defended.

In Canada the strains of war did not produce revolutionary changes, although, as the Rowell-Sirois Commission pointed out, the Great War did lead to a sharpening of class divisions and "a growing class consciousness in the industrial population" (*Report of the Royal Commission on Dominion-Provincial Relations,* p. 89; hereafter cited as Rowell-Sirois). This situation was partly a result of the vast increase in productive capacity and the corresponding increase in trade union membership, which more than doubled between 1914 and 1919. It was also partly attributable to the fact that the war was to a considerable extent financed through inflation which caused prices and the cost of living to rise more rapidly than average wage rates and also caused profits from industry and property incomes to increase while real wages declined (*ibid.*, p. 99). And as the Commission also noted, in Canada, as in other countries, "the success with which the Dominion Government had organized a peaceful society for combat showed how governments could alter the conditions of economic and social life" (*ibid.*, p. 90). If men could be conscripted, why not wealth?

World War I also temporarily upset the precarious political balance between English-speaking Canada and French-speaking Canada, as the conscription crisis created new tensions between Canada's two nations. Generally, however, the country's war losses were regarded as a heroic contribution to a just, and finally victorious, cause which was partially compensated for by the winning of *de facto* political autonomy from Britain. Yet ultimately the collapse of the nineteenth-century world economic system as a result of the war was to have disastrous consequences for Canada's National Policy.

### *The North Atlantic Triangle and the National Policy*

In the nineteenth century Canadian development occurred within the context of a national policy designed to integrate Canada within the North Atlantic economy at a time of British expansion. Clearly the external conditions, particularly those existing in Britain, were of major importance, but Canadian politicians and businessmen were instrumental in developing transportation networks and creating the conditions that would assist the inflow of large quantities of capital.

As Vernon Fowke argued ("The National Policy – Old and New," p. 243), the object of the national policy for a century following the 1820's was the creation of "a new frontier of investment opportunities for the commercial and financial interests of the St. Lawrence area."

The St. Lawrence merchants and bankers saw the river and the Great Lakes as a means by which they could play a middleman role between markets in Britain and the resources of the interior of North America. The timber trade, which opened up much of Ontario and Quebec, and the expansion of agriculture in Upper Canada, both took place within the framework of British preferential tariffs. The merchants also hoped to tap the trade to Europe from the western U.S. When the British government redefined its imperial policy in the mid-nineteenth century, the Montreal merchants panicked, asked for reciprocity of trade with the States, and even considered the seductions of annexation. (See G.N. Tucker, *The Canadian Commercial Revolution, 1845–51.*)

By the 1860's there were renewed hopes for the maintenance of the national policy. The national policy could be revived by the creation of a unified political system: "The federal government was created an agent within the framework of the first national policy ..." (Fowke, "The National Policy – Old and New," p. 245). The National Policy of the 1870's was the necessary economic complement to the British North America Act. It was part of that continuing national policy which was constituted by the "group of policies and instruments which were designed to transform the British North American territories of the mid-nineteenth century into a political and economic unit" (V. Fowke, *The National Policy and the Wheat Economy,* p. 8).

Clifford Sifton, as Minister of the Interior from 1896–1905, was a powerful force in the administration of the National Policy. His views exemplified the difference between liberalism in Canada and the laissez-faire liberalism of Britain and the United States. As J.W. Dafoe explained it, Sifton "was no believer in the principle of *laissez-faire*. He held the view that a government, by conscious and premeditated acts, could change conditions, re-adjust the balance between the sections and control the national prosperity" (J.W. Dafoe, *Clifford Sifton in Relation to his Times,* quoted in W.L. Morton, *The Progressive Party in Canada,* p. 7, n. 5). The Canadian government used a mixture of government grants and market forces in providing transportation and land settlement. The CPR of course received huge amounts of government financial support and large tracts of land, which they were able to sell at market prices to settlers. The government initiated a free-homestead policy by means of which one-quarter sections, entered after the payment of a fee, could be appropriated after a period of several years' settlement. Ultimately, however, more land was sold than was alienated through free-homesteading. (On the railroads see G.P. de T. Glazebrook, *A History of Transportation,* and H.A. Innis, *A History of the Canadian Pacific Railway.* On land settlements see Chester Martin, *Dominion Lands Policy.*)

The use of tariff policy was also seen to be fundamental in establishing some Canadian control over economic development. The British government had resisted this at first, although circumstances in Canada required modification of British policies. The Navigation Acts, for example, were a dead letter from the 1830's with respect to Canadian-American sea trade. The Act of Union reserved to the Imperial Government the right to regulate tariffs, but the Canadian legislature gradually established independence in this respect and Galt's tariff of 1859 has been seen as a "declaration of fiscal independence" (O.J. McDiarmid, *Commercial Policy in the Canadian Economy*, p. 83). The National Policy tariff was established to assist manufacturing in central Canada and to link central Canada with the West and the Maritimes.

Thus the ultimate economic goal of Confederation was the creation of a continent-wide trading system. The 1867 Act assumes growth based on the development of the new western agricultural regions, industrialization, large-scale immigration, and a continuation of the commercial system of the British Empire. The powers necessary to guide such development were conferred upon the Ottawa government. Macdonald's National Policy of 1879 showed how the government was to be used in promoting such development.

The achievement of Confederation had not been a signal for immediate economic development. Canada was affected by a world-wide depression which began in 1873. (One of the consequences of this depression was the new phase in the history of imperialism discussed above.) In Canada the 1870's witnessed the development of the theory of a national policy of economic integration and industrialization. The Budget Speech of March 1879 which called for high tariffs put the point clearly: "the time has arrived when we are to decide whether we will simply be hewers of wood and drawers of water" (Rowell-Sirois, p. 51).

Given the nature of Canada's economy and the underlying world conditions, the imposition of tariffs, even with a western settlement policy and the creation of a transcontinental railroad, was not enough to produce rapid growth. Accordingly, emigration to the States continued at a high level in the 1870's and 1880's. It could be said, however, that the basis for industrialization was being laid in this period. (See Easterbrook and Aitken, *Canadian Economic History* and Tom Naylor, *A History of Canadian Business,* vol. 2.)

The economic turning point was 1896, when the new gold from South Africa, the Klondike, Alaska, and northern Ontario contributed to a new rise in prices. The renewed exports of capital from the United Kingdom and the lowered transportation costs gave rise to the "Wheat Boom" period which lasted until 1913. There are two points about this boom which should be noted. The first is that the Maritimes failed to share in the boom. In fact, "The tariff policy imposed a drastic change in the conditions under which the Maritimes had developed" (Rowell-Sirois, p. 78). The only beneficiaries there were the Nova Scotian steel and coal industries. The second point is that the prosperity of the rest of the Canadian economy was conditional upon the export of wheat.

In fact a close study of the economic mechanisms involved in the wheat boom shows the early emergence of weaknesses in the national policy. It also points to the complications introduced by the asymmetry of centre-periphery schemes of development. It illustrates how an international situation could be created in which, as a result of shifts in the relationship between two imperialist powers, namely the United States and Britain, a dependent economy like Canada's could be transferred from one empire to another.

In 1900 foreign capital invested in Canada amounted to about $1200 million. From 1900–13, the period of the wheat boom, a further $2500 million was invested in Canada, of which about $1750 million came from Britain and about $630 million from the United States. But *how* did this massive transfer of funds enter Canada and what were the implications? (This question is the subject of the fundamentally important study by Jacob Viner, *Canada's Balance of International Indebtedness, 1900–13.* The above figures for capital imports are taken from this source.)

The classical analysis of such transfers (following Henry Thornton and John Stuart Mill, against the authority of Ricardo) suggests that prices would increase in Canada relative to prices in Britain, that Canadian imports would increase and exports decrease, and that thus Britain would actually send the capital to Canada in the form of goods. But what actually happened? Exports did not in fact fall, though here there is the problem of the general economic expansion overlying the relative price movements. But consider which commodity exports increased. Eighty per cent of the increase in exports by value (more by quantity) from 1900–13 was accounted for by the following commodities: wheat, flour, pulp and paper, copper, nickel, aluminum and asbestos. The price rise of this group of commodities was below the average price rise for this period (Viner, pp. 264ff). There was an increase in exports of some manufactured goods, but this was mostly in automobiles from Ford to the British Empire.

As Viner notes (p. 269), "in the large the maintenance of the volume of Canadian exports in the face of rising costs of production was made possible only by the discovery and exploitation of new low cost natural resources."

The borrowed capital was transferred to Canada mainly in the form of increased commodity imports. Approximately 30–40 per cent of the commodity imports were capital goods. (*ibid.*, p. 276; see Table LVI). So far the result is not surprising. Foreign investment leads to an outflow of resources and an inflow of manufactured goods. But the case is more complicated. British funds, which were made available to Canadians by the flotation of loans in London, were used to buy foreign currency in New York, which was in turn used to pay for increased imports from the States (*ibid.*, p. 280).

The adjustment of the British balance of payments then took place through increased British exports to the States – or, in an even more circuitous fashion, through increased British exports to Latin America or Asia, paid for by exports from these regions to the States.

What this meant was that the United States could become a major investor in Canada at a time when it was still a net debtor in the whole international system. This made possible the growth of branch plants in Canada, while at the same time the United States was increasing its exports of manufactured goods to Canada. In fact the two were connected as the branch plants bought American equipment and machinery.

The wheat boom period, with its peculiar consequences, lasted until 1913. The boom broke as interest rates rose and the price level of Canadian exports began to fall. It was war that halted the depression by reviving the market for wheat and other foodstuff exports. In addition, war demand gave a considerable boost to the northern resource industries: pulp and paper, hydro power, and the mining industry.[3] The war also produced a rapid increase in manufacturing output, encouraged by the disruption of imports from Central Europe and the decline in British exports. The high cost of ocean shipping further enabled Canadian industry to secure a larger share of the home market. (Rowell-Sirois, p. 91). The increase in production paid for the cost of the war and also met the interest charges on a debt that could no longer be financed by foreign borrowing.

One clear consequence of the war was the hastening of the re-orientation of the Canadian economy towards the United States. As British investment fell, provinces and municipalities turned to New York for financing. Canadian banking, as well as Canadian industry, was firmly locked into the American orbit.

The short-run effect of the ending of the war was an immediate and severe postwar depression. The national income dropped 14 per cent from 1920 to 1921. The solution was sought in an attempt to restore the prewar conditions of international trade and capital movements and for a while Canadian exports began to rise again. The war had created a strong market for Canadian wheat, and between 1922 and 1926 Canada supplied 38 per cent of the world's wheat exports (compared with 12 per cent during 1900–14). But this export boom began to weaken by 1925 as European production recovered and as an increasing overproduction of foodstuffs led to tariff barriers in one country after another. Thus the second wheat boom remained a major factor throughout the 1920's, but it was no longer the overriding factor it once had been.

It was in fact in the 1920's that the decisive weakening of the National Policy occurred:

> The national integration (achieved through wheat), which tied the country together by East-West bonds of trade and opportunity was weakened as Central Canada and British Columbia felt the direct and competing tug of export demand on their regional resources. New economic frontiers, the exploitation of which was of primary interest to Ontario and Quebec (and to a lesser extent Manitoba), developed on the Pre-Cambrian Shield – where water power, base metals and pulp and paper came into their own, – and began to usurp the place of the old national frontier in the West. (Rowell-Sirois, p. 112)

The export of pulp and paper and non-ferrous metals rose to 30 per cent of the total exports in 1929 compared with 19 per cent in 1920 (*ibid.*, p. 116). A second area of expansion was the creation of a new transportation network based on the automobile.

Of fundamental importance was the fact that the central provinces had now had their growth linked to exports outside of Canada, rather than to exports to Western Canada, as had been envisaged by the national policy. The growth of resource exports had also increasingly meant growth tied to the United States. This did not, at this time, mean a check to the growth of manufacturing in Central Canada, or to the regional inequalities in the distribution of wealth in Canada. In Quebec manufacturing grew with an emphasis on consumer goods. In Ontario there was a boom in the durable goods and machinery industries, but the exports of many of these were tied to the imperial preference tariff system.

Canada's recovery, however, depended on an international recovery and the ultimate inability of the capitalist countries to put back together the international economy of the pre-1914 days was demonstrated in the depression of the 1930's. A major crisis in world agriculture and raw materials and a breakdown in the network of capital flows produced a massive setback to world trade. Between 1929 and 1931 the value of world trade fell by 42 per cent and continued to fall until 1933. (Rowell-Sirois, p. 141. Half the fall was accounted for by value, half by volume.) The reaction to the crisis by the producers of manufactured goods was to restrict output and maintain prices. In primary industries the consequence was increased output and sharply reduced prices. The problem of trade balance under such conditions was insoluble. The gold standard was insupportable for primary producing countries such as Australia, New Zealand, and most of Latin America. The collapse of an Austrian bank, the Kredit-Anstalt, in the spring of 1931 led to a wave of financial crises, and eventually this succession of events struck at the currency of the largest import market in the world. In September 1931 the United Kingdom went off the gold standard. *Macdonald's National Policy was at an end.* (See Rowell-Sirois, chap. 6.)

Canada had effectively gone off the gold standard in 1928. That the Canadian dollar did not follow the decline of the pound was evidence that the National Policy had long ago been seriously weakened by the increasing attachment of Canada to the U.S. economy. Canada did not become part of the sterling bloc which rapidly emerged after the floating of the pound in 1931.

Throughout the period after World War I there had been an increasing weight of evidence to show that Canada's independence from Britain was matched by a growing assimilation to the United States. Mackenzie King's signing of the 1935 reciprocal trade agreement between Canada and the United States was symbolic. It formalized the policy of continentalism. Economically the major effect of the treaty was to stimulate the import of manufactured goods from the United States while Canada "reciprocated" with the export of primary products and whisky. (See J.B. Brebner, *The North Atlantic Triangle,* p. 314.)

As Creighton and others have noted, the 1940 Ogdensburg Agreement marked a further turning of the screw. In addition to having become a branch plant dependency, Canada was to become a U.S. military satellite. (See D. Creighton, "The Decline and Fall of the Empire of the St. Lawrence." Also Jim Laxer, "The Political Economy of Canada.")

The national policy had become the victim of changing imperial relationships, the decline of Britain, and the rise of the United States. As one historian has pointed out (Hugh Aitken, "Defensive Expansion: The State and Economic Growth in Canada," p. 217), it is ironic that the St. Lawrence Seaway illustrates Canada's satellitic role vis-à-vis the United States and Great Britain. The Seaway was originally thought of as a means of enabling Canada to capture and control part of the transit trade between Great Britain and the American mid-west; the idea reflected Canada's role as an economic satellite of the former. In its final form, however, the Seaway is largely facilitating the export of Canadian raw materials to the United States. The St. Lawrence River, throughout most of Canada's history a symbol of a dominant orientation toward Europe, now served to strengthen Canada's economic ties to the United States.

## Notes

1. There are many scholars who are suspicious of the term "imperialism," perhaps because of the political context in which many of the arguments were first developed. In England the discussion was opened in 1902 by J.A. Hobson's *Imperialism* which argued that capitalism was being distorted by arms dealers and financiers. In continental Europe the subject was hotly debated within the socialist movement at the turn of the century. The best-known work to emerge from the debate was Rosa Luxemburg's *Accumulation of Capital* (1913). The argument was taken up by Bukharin in *Imperialism and World Economy* (1915), an essay which appeared with an introduction by Lenin. In 1916 Lenin himself wrote what is probably still the best-known analysis of the subject, *Imperialism: The Highest State of Capitalism.* (For recent work on the subject, see V.G. Kiernan, *Marxism and Imperialism* and M. Barratt Brown, *The Economics of Imperialism*).

Rosa Luxemburg's analysis of imperialism is rooted in a theory of underconsumption. She stresses the revolutionary upheavals caused as traditional ways are forcibly changed by the expansion of capitalism to "backward" communities. This argument has the merit of explaining an important aspect of the European world expansion and at the same time explaining the significance of peasant wars. One of the limitations, however, is that Luxemburg assumes that expansion occurs only to non-capitalist economies, obscuring the equally important point that imperialism can also involve expansion into societies which are already capitalist.

The context for Lenin's writings on imperialism was the catastrophe of World War I. As he wrote in 1915: "There can be no concrete historical analysis of the present war, if that analysis does not have for its basis a full understanding of the nature of imperialism, both from its economic and political aspects." Lenin identified imperialism with a new stage in the development of capitalism. Imperialism was "a system of the economic relations of modern highly developed, mature, and over-ripe capitalism." An imperialist system had become necessary because, by the end of the nineteenth century, "commodity exchange had created such an internationalisation of economic relations and such a vast increase in large-scale production, that free competition began to be replaced by monopoly." Lenin thus linked imperialism with monopoly capitalism, as had Bukharin. Both saw imperialism as a continuation of the process of the concentration and centralization of capital which had been explained by Marx. And beginning before World War I, but hastened by the war, had been the growth of the state as an organizer of industry and a critical agent in imperialism.

Thus imperialism was a product of capitalist growth, and, as Lenin showed, it was the uneven development of capitalism in the various countries that provoked war among the imperialist powers:

> The Capitalists divide the world, not out of any particular malice, but because the degree of concentration which has been reached forces them to adopt this method in order to obtain profits. And they divide it "in proportion to capital", "in proportion to strength", because there cannot be any other method of division under commodity production and capitalism. But strength varies with the degree of economic and political development.

The changing strength of the imperialist powers led to a redistribution of colonial areas which could not always be solved by "diplomacy" or even by minor colonial wars. Lenin recognized that colonial policy and imperialism had existed before the monopoly stage of capitalism and even before capitalism. But he was concerned to identify the specific features of imperialist monopoly capitalism and World War I.

The limitations of Lenin's arguments are in the problems of identifying precise turning points in economic development (see M. Barratt Brown, above, pp. 183-200), and in an overemphasis on the German pattern of development. The strength of the analysis lies in stressing the link between expansion and a particular organization of capital.

**2.** On changing themes of nationalism see E.J. Hobsbawm, *The Age of Capital.* The link between democracy and national survival had in fact already been suggested in France at the time of the revolution and again at the time of the Paris Commune. The Commune showed the possibility that the defence of the country could be carried on by the working class in opposition to the upper classes who had been unable or unwilling to defend France from German occupation. In France the national hegemony of the bourgeoisie has been threatened twice again by German occupation.

**3.** The case of the nickel industry provides an interesting example of political development. See H.G.J. Aitken, "The Changing Structure of the Canadian Economy," and H.V. Nelles, *The Politics of Development,* chap. 9.

# THREE
# The U.S. Empire and Internationalism

> The maxims of conquest are not always to be distinguished from those of self-defence. ... Rome never avowed any other maxims of conquest; and she everywhere sent her insolent armies, under the specious pretence of procuring to herself and her allies a lasting peace, which she alone would reserve the power to disturb. (Adam Ferguson, *An Essay on the History of Civil Society,* part 3, section 5)

As a result of its history as a refuge for millions of emigrants from Europe, the United States has often been thought to have a social history profoundly different from that of nineteenth-century Europe. And in the course of its ascent to international supremacy, its ideologues have usually, though not always, eschewed the imperialist rhetoric of European spokesmen. The Monroe Doctrine justified "defensive expansionism," and later U.S. expansionists frequently disguised their imperial ambitions by calling for "Open Door" policies in opposition to the formal colonial rule of other capitalist powers. Since 1917 arguments about the need to contain communist expansion have provided an excuse for U.S. expansion.

There is no doubt that the image of America has been tarnished in recent years as racial conflict, the war against Vietnam, and the sordid behaviour of U.S. corporate executives and government officials, including presidents, has revealed on television screens around the world some of the horrifying truths about U.S. society. But there has been a tendency to ascribe this change of the American dream to the American nightmare to a sudden fall from grace. It is probably true that, for much of its history, the United States has been more or less spontaneously seen by millions as the example of a free and democratic society. But it has also been true that the major product of American advertising has always been America itself. This was particularly noticeable in the period after World War II when a conscious campaign was inaugurated to sustain the image of the United States as natural leader of the "free world."

There were two main points in this campaign. First, it presented the United States as a model of a democratic society from which other countries could learn to erase the errors of the past and thus avoid perils in the future. Second, it attempted to ingrain the view that it could only be irrationality on the part of foreigners to refuse to welcome the "American way of life." Some Americans recognized that they would have to overcome resistance in other countries, but they entered into the struggle in the spirit of missionaries setting out to exorcize the irrational.

One of the barriers that Americans frequently encountered was the nationalism of others who were not sure that the American presence in their country was always so benign. This point was clearly seen, for example, by Mr. Parker, chairman of the Parker Pen Company: "Today I believe it is America's manifest role to extend the fruits of private enterprise throughout the world. The private sector of the American economy is the logical leader of this crusade. It is our manifest obligation to lift ox-and-plow cultures into the 20th century, but we must face realistically the certainty that nationalism in emerging countries will resist the American presence." (Quoted in S. Hymer, "Partners in development," p. 10. Parker's statement was made in 1968).

In the 1950's some of the assumptions of American policy were set out in the modestly titled book by Professor W.W. Rostow, *The Stages of Growth: A Non-Communist Manifesto.* One of the enemies of the American pattern of progress was identified as "reactive nationalism," a perversion of the "legitimate" desires for independence which of course could be fostered by "internationalism" and "co-operation." It seemed that nationalism was all right so long as the Americans defined it for you. In fact in defining the interests of the world, the Americans left very little room for the nationalism of others. A foreign policy study produced in 1955 made this point clear. Concerning the underdeveloped countries the report said:

> The U.S. cannot validly claim to speak for these other civilizations in setting goals and strategy for foreign policy, as it can within limits for the Western Community of which it is the natural leader. The U.S. does have, however, the right and duty to try to define and to protect vital Western security and economic interests. ... The moral duty to respect the freedom and self-determination of these other societies ... does not require the West to surrender its own security and its truly vital economic interests in the name of a self-determination which insists upon expressing itself exclusively in a national form. ...

This extract is taken from the Study Group of the Woodrow Wilson Foundation and the National Planning Association, *The Political Economy of American Foreign Policy,* p. 224. The writers of this study suggested that a general aim of development should be to win over the "native intellectual and middleclass groups who might otherwise supply leadership and cadres to subversive movements. Lack of organic social functions and adequate opportunities make these groups highly susceptible to communism or irresponsible nationalism" (*ibid.,* pp. 225–26).

What American opinion did not wish to contemplate, however, was the possibility that resistance to the American presence in other countries was not the result of irrationality, but rather the result of the perception that the United States had long been an aggressive imperial power, pursuing its own self-interest behind a cloak of benevolence and internationalism.

### *The Growth of the U.S. Empire*

It is commonly argued that the American War of Independence was the first round of the liberal revolutions that shook Europe and the Americas until the mid-nineteenth century. (See R.R. Palmer, *The Age of the Democratic Revolution.*) And there is no doubt that the revolutionary liberalism of Thomas Paine, as exhibited in his immensely popular *Common Sense,* had a powerful effect both within the American colonies and elsewhere. It is also true, however, that the revolutionary and international liberalism of the

American revolution was integrated with, and increasingly subordinated to, the nationalism of the newly United States. (This was also the case in revolutionary France, although the defeat of France in 1815 limited its development. It was also true of the revolutionary socialism of the USSR in the twentieth century.) In the United States the revolutionary liberalism merged with a pre-liberal religious messianism which reinforced the belief that a new world was being created.

As William Appleman Williams has shown, the United States of America was not founded entirely on liberal principles. ( See W.A. Williams, *The Contours of American History*.) An essential point is that the early history of the United States was formed in the context of British mercantilism and the struggle for independence was a defensive reaction to a new phase of British imperialism. The mercantilist system had led to the creation of a colonial gentry who largely accepted the colonial framework. Even in 1775 Benjamin Franklin said that he had heard no expressions of a desire for separation from Britain. The colonial gentry, however, could not accept the new imperialist claims, and drawing upon popular support, they led the revolution to establish a new mercantilist system with the American colonies at the centre instead of at the periphery. The extension of U.S. power took place first within the North American continent, justified by the ideology of "Manifest Destiny." The United States rapidly excluded other imperial powers from limiting its expansion. The 1803 Louisiana Purchase, the War of 1812 with Canada, the Oregon dispute of the 1840's, the 1846–48 Mexican War, and the 1867 Alaska Purchase were all part of this policy. The U.S. government also annexed western land in 1868. It is not surprising that British and Canadian governments considered that unification of the British North American possessions was a necessary defensive step.

The ideology of expansion remained prominent in U.S. government circles. In 1860, William Seward, U.S. secretary of state under Lincoln, had noted that "an ingenious and ambitious people" were building Canada. He went on "it is very well that you are building excellent states to be hereafter admitted into the American Union" (quoted in W. LaFeber: *The New Empire*, p. 25). What could be called the "ripe fruit" theory of Canada has been held by a succession of U.S. politicians. It was still common around the turn of the century, as witness the utterances of James "Jingo Jim" Blaine, secretary of state in the 1880's and 90's and, in the early 20th century, those of President Taft. In the early 1890's Blaine proposed a commercial union of the two countries. The offer was refused by the Conservative government but U.S. interest in integrating Canada did not wane. Governor General Lord Minto wrote of this period that, notwithstanding British sentiment about "Anglo-saxon" kinship, he was not surprised at the Canadians' general dislike of the Yankees: "What the Canadian sees and hears is constant Yankee bluff and swagger and that eventually he means to possess Canada for himself" (quoted in R. Craig Brown and Ramsay Cook, *Canada 1896–1921*, p. 28). It seems likely that Taft's constant references to the inevitability of Canada's annexation by the United States contributed to the Conservative win in the 1911 "no trade nor truck with the Yankees" election. (See J.B. Brebner, *North Atlantic Triangle*, pp. 253, 274.)

The victory of the north in the U.S. Civil War is considered by many Canadian historians to have been a factor in the desire for Confederation. The Civil War revealed the extent to which the developing industrial capitalism in the north had become incompatible, within the same country, with the colonial, plantation and slave society of the south. The south was to a considerable extent still linked to the United Kingdom, and the Civil War can be seen as the second round in the War of Independence.[1]

By the late nineteenth century, U.S industrialization had reached a stage where expansion outside the North American continent had become necessary. In 1897 Senator Albert Beveridge articulated this need:

> American factories are making more than the American people can use; American soil is producing more than they can consume. Fate has written our policy for us; the trade of the world must and shall be ours. ... American law, American order, American civilization, and the American flag will plant themselves on shores hitherto bloody and benighted, but by the agencies of God henceforth to be made beautiful and bright. (Quoted in Claude Julien, *America's Empire*, p. 420)

This view was characteristic of the response to the depressions of the 1880's and 1890's. The growth of the industrial working class and such manifestations of class conflict as the great railroad strike of 1877, the eight-hour movement of the 1880's, the May Day strike movement, and, in the 1890's, the Homestead, Coeur d'Alène, and Pullman strikes had encouraged many in the States to see the advantages of a new imperialist expansion. In the 1890's troops were used on more than three hundred occasions to quell disturbances. An English observer, James Dicey, noted that American thought on expansion was following British in recognizing that "democratic institutions are no longer a panacea for the cure of social discontents" (quoted in V.G. Kiernan, "Imperialism, American and European," p. 109).

In addition to using many of the racial arguments for empire that were common in Europe, American spokesmen also modified the ideology of imperialism to suit their own conditions. Frederick Jackson Turner's "frontier thesis" was used to explain that American democracy and prosperity in the past had been the result of expansion across the continent. With the closing of the western frontier it was necessary to find a "new frontier." (This argument was consciously resurrected in 1960 as the U.S. attempted to outmanoeuvre the USSR and a resurgent Europe).

In 1895 Senator Henry Cabot Lodge argued: "We have a record of conquest, colonization, and expansion, unequalled by any people in the 19th century. We are not to be curbed now." (Williams, *The Contours of American History,* p. 345) Lodge also made clear the meaning of the Monroe Doctrine: "The doctrine has no bearing on the extension of the United States, but simply holds that no European power shall establish itself in the Americas or interfere with American governments." (G. Stedman Jones, "The History of U.S. Imperialism")

The existence of the Dominion of the North was presumably an affront to Lodge's interpretation of the Monroe Doctrine, particularly as the United States was now reaching the stage where it no longer needed to interpret the doctrine within the confines of the Pax Britannica. But perhaps Lodge thought that problem could be dealt with by gently shaking the tree.

Lodge would have had some reason to feel that way. The British government had never been overly zealous in its defence of Canadian interests against U.S. encroachments. For example, the Atlantic colonies had suffered from U.S. penetration of the British West Indies, and in the many fishing disputes U.S. interests had generally prevailed over the British government. It was true that British naval policy in Canada, the Caribbean, and Central America was not consonant with the Monroe Doctrine, but by this time the British government was aware that it could not maintain its global hegemony. A tacit decision to avoid conflict with the United States was indicated by the reduction of bases at Halifax and Esquimault and the closing of dockyards in Jamaica. Both the West Indian and the North American squadrons were abolished. In the 1890's Britain quickly bowed to U.S. pressure for arbitration of the boundary dispute between Venezuela and British Guiana and also gave up her rights in the Panama Canal. (See M. Howard, *The Continental Commitment*, pp. 29–30.)

Few American expansionists have been so outspoken as Lodge. In the 1890's, as now, imperialist doctrine was frequently cloaked in the rhetoric of world order and peace. In 1893 the U.S. magazine *Harpers* set the keynote for a long succession of American speakers: "If we have fighting to do, it will be fighting to keep the peace" (Williams, *The Tragedy of American Diplomacy,* p. 26). The statement of President Cleveland on Cuba in 1896 has become a familiar story: "Either the rebellion must be ended or this government will be compelled to protect its own interests and those of its citizens, which are coincident with those of humanity and civilization generally, by resorting to such measures as will promptly restore to the Island the blessings of peace" (*ibid.*, p. 31). When faced with such statements we should remember that the note sent by the U.S. government to Spain in the 1890's is clearer as to the motives of U.S. intervention:

> The extraordinary, because direct and not merely theoretical or sentimental, interests of the U.S. in the Cuban situation cannot be ignored. ... Not only are our citizens largely concerned in the ownership of property and in the industrial and commercial ventures ... but the chronic condition of trouble causes disturbance in the social and political conditions of our own peoples. ... A continuous irritation within our borders injuriously affects the normal functions of business and tends to delay the condition of prosperity to which this country is entitled. (G. Stedman Jones, p. 227)

In the late nineteenth century, U.S. capital and U.S. government influence moved southwards to Cuba, Venezuela, Mexico, Puerto Rico, Santo Domingo, Salvador, Colombia, and beyond. They also moved westwards, using Midway and Hawaii as stepping stones, to the other side of the Pacific. Much of this expansion was to secure markets or sources of tropical products. But there had been an important structural change in the U.S. economy, which was to have particular significance for the northward expansion.

The growth of the U.S. economy in this period was marked by the appearance of large, vertically integrated, centralized enterprises which dominated the major industries. In the 1880's and 1890's over 5,000 companies were consolidated into about 300 trusts (See C. Tugendhat, *The Multinationals*, p. 35). More and more industries were characterized by oligopoly as a succession of depressions at the end of the nineteenth century led to the concentration of economic power.

It was at this time that the United States began to export manufactured goods in large quantities (Magdoff, *The Age of Imperialism,* p. 35). And it was at this time that she began to "export" capital in the form of direct investment. She began to establish direct control of mineral supplies and also of manufacturing through the creation of branch plants. It was the concentration of industry in the United States that led to branch-plant investment as a new mode of competition became necessary. (This point was made by S. Hymer, *The International Operations of National Firms,* esp. chap. 3.)

Williams suggests that the new industrial corporations generally exercised a dominant influence in U.S. foreign policy, except with regard to Asia where some banking houses, such as the House of Morgan, maintained control. For the corporations trade did not mean simply the exchange of commodities. It meant the control of raw materials and the control of markets for American exports. (See W. A. Williams, "The Large Corporation and American Foreign Policy.")

Canada was an early target for this corporate expansion. By the end of 1934 there were 1,350 U.S. corporations active in Canada: 5 per cent of them began operations before 1900, 11 per cent were established from 1900 to 1909, 22 per cent from 1910 to 1919, 36 per cent from 1920 to 1929, and 26 per cent from 1930 to 1934. (See J.B. Brebner, *North Atlantic Triangle,* pp. 243–44, quoting the 1936 study by H. Marshall, F.A. Southard, and K.W. Taylor.) By the 1930's more than a quarter of manufacturing in Canada, and also of mining and smelting was controlled by U.S. corporations. (See K. Levitt, *Silent Surrender,* p. 61.) U.S. investors owned about 21 per cent of foreign investment in Canada in 1913. By 1926 their share had risen to 53 per cent.

### *"Multinational" Corporations and the U.S. Empire*

Each imperial centre has its own method of integrating peripheral countries into the empire. The method will be determined by the requirements of the centre country and also by the potential of the peripheral country. This means that imperialism does not always proceed by the same mechanisms, even if access to raw materials and control of markets may remain as consistent aims. We should not assume that the integrative mechanisms of British imperialism in the late nineteenth century were the same as those of the German imperialism of the same time. And neither should we assume that the U.S. empire is integrated by the patterns established by either Britain or Germany, or any other country.

In fact the "multinational" corporation has played a critical role in the formation of the U.S. imperial system, and thus its procedures have been different from past patterns of imperial expansion. In 1914 approximately 90 per cent of all international capital movements took the form of portfolio investment. By the 1970's however, approximately 75 per cent of capital outflows from industrial countries were in the form of direct investment. This change in the world economy has had profound implications for Canada for two reasons. First, it has meant that a major part of all investment in Canada has been controlled by U.S. corporations; and second, that a very large proportion of all U.S. foreign investment is in Canada. The consequence of the latter point is that Canada has become the most valuable peripheral country in the U.S. empire. The consequence of the first point is the direct control of large sectors of the Canadian economy, not simply by owners who reside outside the country, but by U.S. corporations whose Canadian holdings are part of their larger corporate structure. Foreign control through portfolio investment is not negligible. It includes such major corporations as Inco, Falconbridge, and Alcan, all of which are controlled by American investors. But it is the so-called multinational corporation that dominates the Canadian economy and has integrated the Canadian economy into the U.S. empire.

There are frequent assertions that the corporations have now outgrown the nation-state and have become a new international agency. It is suggested that capital is now international, and the multinational corporations are no longer clearly associated with any particular state. But even the largest corporations, which like to view the whole world as their sphere of operations, cannot dispense with national governments because of the essential services that they render. Multinational corporations require governments to maintain capitalist social relations of production through property laws and legislation for control of the labour force. Multinational corporations in addition require governments to establish regulations for foreign trade and capital movements, even if at times they individually find it convenient to evade these regulations. Multinational corporations rely on their home governments to represent their interests with foreign governments, even to the point of propping up friendly foreign governments that can no longer depend on the support of their own people. The corporations may call on their home governments to discredit, and even help remove, unfriendly foreign governments that no longer represent the interests of the multinational corporations.

Of course it is true that the rise of the multinational corporation has had profound implications for nation states. Politics is largely about economic questions, and the growth of the multinationals has had direct political implications. The role of these corporations has been to remove much economic and political control from the governments of peripheral countries. (Kari Levitt, in *Silent Surrender*, has characterized the multinationals as agents of a "new mercantilism." On the political implications, see Abraham Rotstein, *The Precarious Homestead*, chap. 3. Even major European countries have felt the effects of this development. See, for example, Jean-Jacques Servan-Schreiber, *The American Challenge*.)

The effect of the multinationals has not been to internationalize the control of capital. The effect has been to "denationalize" large areas of the life of the foreign countries where they operate. In many countries, including Canada, control of technological development, dominance in financial markets and labour markets, and the promotion of market place ideologies has come under the control of U.S. multinational corporations. George Ball, a prominent U.S. government spokesman and a believer in the "internationalization" of economies, has told Canadians that the "inevitable substantial economic integration" of Canada and the United States "will require for its full realization a progressively expanding area of common political decision" (A. Rotstein, *The Precarious Homestead,* p. 43).

Within the economic system of multinational corporations it is clear that U.S. corporations are dominant. (On the significance of non-American multinationals, see R. Rowthorn and S. Hymer, *International Big Business, 1957-1967.*) The U.S. corporations are partly dominant because of their greater size and financial power which can lead to technological advantages. But also important is the role of the U.S. government. The government is an important market, both military and civilian, and its power can be used in arranging tax privileges and tariff concessions and in general giving support in negotiations with other governments. Also of considerable importance has been the ability of U.S. corporations to attract skilled workers and scientists, trained in other countries, into their employ both in the United States and abroad.

In the period beginning with the Second World War, the U.S. government has played a significant role in promoting the influence of U.S. multinationals, and this has frequently taken the form of direct confrontations with other governments. The war period offered many opportunities for Washington to aid the extension of U.S. corporate control and the postwar definition of U.S. national security enhanced this activity. For example, the American Viscose Corporation, which was the world's largest rayon producer and was in fact the American subsidiary of the British corporation Courtaulds, was "hounded in Congress and the Press until in 1941 the U.S. Government insisted it should be sold at a knock-down price as a condition of lend-lease to Britain." (Tugendhat, p. 39. The politics of dependence are revealed in Churchill's remark that Lend Lease was "the most unsordid act in history.")

In 1946 U.S. Secretary of War Forrestal wrote to Secretary of State Marshall that it was "of the utmost importance to the national interest and security that all communications facilities in the western hemisphere be owned by hemispheric interests and, if possible, by companies controlled by citizens of the United States" (quoted in Anthony Sampson, *The Sovereign State of ITT,* p. 44).

It has been revealed by a U.S. Senate Select Committee on Intelligence that Forrestal went further. In 1947 he asked RCA Global, ITT World Communications, and Western Union International to supply the U.S. government with copies of most of the messages they carried. The companies were offered immunity from prosecution and they complied, turning over paper-tapes, microfilm, and magnetic tapes to the National Security Agency and other intelligence agencies.

Expansion into Europe was a main aim of U.S. policy in the 1940's. In 1901 there had been 37 subsidiaries engaged in manufacturing in Europe, the United Kingdom, Germany, and France being the preferred countries. The numbers grew steadily, reaching 84 by 1919, 226 by 1929, and 335 by 1939. Then from 1950 to 1959 the number increased from 363 to 677 and by 1967 had reached 1438. (See R. Vernon, *Sovereignty at Bay,* Table 2, p. 68.) And after World War II, U.S. companies were encouraged to expand into Europe:

> The U.S. government hoped that a flow of company investment funds would reduce the level of official loans and grants needed to launch Europe's economic recovery. It exhorted companies to go overseas, and took practical steps to help them by negotiating double taxation agreements with a large number of governments, and by guaranteeing their investments against restraints on the repartriation of profits. ... At first progress was slow. Companies were happy to invest in Canada, which was near, politically stable and prosperous. But Europe was another matter. The Soviet threat, political instability, and closer government regulation of economic and industrial affairs than was customary in North America combined to deter many companies from crossing the Atlantic. It needed time for businessmen to accept that Europe's recovery was firmly based, and its growth potential worth taking risks for. (Tugendhat, pp. 49-50)

Thus the rapid growth of U.S. corporations has created a new type of imperialism, in which even highly industrialized capitalist economies have been subjected to relative degrees of dependence. The multinational corporation has become "the American Trojan

Horse." (The point was made by French political scientist Maurice Duverger in *Le Monde* 29/30 October 1967. See Ernest Mandel, *Europe vs. America,* p. 154. In 1963 de Gaulle's minister of information, Alain Peyrefitte, had referred to Britain as "America's Trojan Horse," referring to Britain's attempt to join the European community.) The multinational corporation in fact plays an additional part as an integrative mechanism of the American empire through its direct role in political financing in other countries, both legal and apparently illegal.

In the first half of the 1970's the major oil companies operating in Canada contributed at least $500,000 annually to the Liberal and the Progressive Conservative parties. Imperial Oil averaged $234,-000 per year, while Gulf Canada was averaging $140,000 per year. (*Maclean's,* 9 February, 1976.) Donations of this magnitude represent a sizeable portion of the receipts of the two parties. These were legal contributions, but investigations by the U.S. Senate subcommittee on multinational corporations have shown a vast network of illegal payoffs and contributions in many countries. Major corporations such as Lockheed Aircraft Corporation and Gulf Oil Corporation used bribes to influence domestic and foreign politicians and government officials. It appears that at least some branches of the U.S. government were aware of these tactics. The Aluminum Company of America, appearing before the U.S. Securities and Exchange Commission, claimed that it made a contribution to a foreign political party at the request of the U.S. ambassador in that country. (For examples, see *Globe and Mail* 16 July, 1976; 2 April, 1976.)

In addition to this kind of behaviour, U.S. corporations can influence the policies of other countries through the actions of those who work for them in their subsidiaries. A Canadian executive, Bruce Willson, explained why, in 1969, he left his job as president of Canadian Bechtel, a subsidiary of the Bechtel Corporation of San Francisco:

> I resigned partly out of frustration at the lack of Canadian control of projects built in this country. ... The power of U.S. controlled corporations to obtain government approvals was very substantial and I didn't want to go along with this. I found conflict between my duties as an officer of Bechtel and my feelings as a Canadian nationalist. ... Bechtel worked within the rules of the

> game, but the game was not in Canada's long term best interests. (Walter Stewart, "Bulldozers Inc.," *Maclean's,* 28 June, 1976, p. 28)

A similar statement was made by the chairman of a U.S.-owned British subsidiary, who explained that, an executive for a multinational corporation;

> must set aside any nationalistic attitudes and appreciate that in the last resort his loyalty must be to the shareholders of the parent company, and he must protect their interests even if it might appear that it is not perhaps in the national interest of the country in which he is operating. Apparent conflicts may occur in such matters as the transfer of funds at a period of national crisis, a transfer of production from one subsidiary to another, or a transfer of export business. (Quoted in Tugendhat, *The Multinationals,* p. 23)[2]

Loyalties undoubtedly become even more confused as multinationals, in addition to creating their own corporate images, extend the values of the country in which they originated. Exxon, for example, considers that the spreading of American business ideology is one of its tasks. As its 1962 Annual Report states: "Our affiliates as corporate citizens communicate their ideas on sound business policy to the people and governments of the countries in which they operate. The public statements made by our management, our written communications, and our advertising seek to emphasize the benefits of free competitive enterprise and private international investment." (Quoted in E. Penrose, *The Large International Firm in Developing Countries,* p. 101. In Canada, Imperial Oil has carried out this policy in its Hockey Night commercials.)

A country that has allowed substantial investment by multinational corporations has given many hostages to fortune. The mere threat to relocate production is a powerful weapon for the multinationals who thus play off various forces against each other. The multinationals blackmail both governments and their own workers by such tactics. The 1970's campaign of the U.S. oil companies in Canada, suggesting that they would not discover our oil for us unless the government behaved responsibly, is only one example in the long history of such behaviour.

It appears that the multinationals also pursue a careful strategy of spreading production potential in different countries. The aim is to make sure that no single foreign group of branch plants is self-sufficient. For example, "the only completely self-sufficient or potentially self-sufficient, country in the IBM network is the U.S. (Tugendhat, p. 155). It has been reported that the president of IBM stopped the development of a small advanced scientific computer by the company's London laboratory in favour of a model developed in the United States. (Vernon, p. 137). Against this reduction of the dangers of nationalization, the multinationals have to duplicate production, or potential, in order to avoid making all foreign operations dependent on any one country. This increases the strength of the company in dealing with strikes at any one of their subsidiaries.

During a 1970 strike Ford actually shipped a critical piece of machinery from the struck plant in Britain to a German subsidiary in order to maintain production. Political pressure is also exerted to this end. In 1971, when workers at the Ford plant in Dagenham, England, were on strike, Henry Ford visited British Prime Minister Heath. Shortly before the meeting Ford announced publicly that "there is nothing at all wrong with Ford of Britain, but with the country. We have got hundreds of millions of pounds invested in Great Britain and we can't recommend any new capital investment in a country constantly dogged with labour problems" (quoted in R.J. Barnet and R.E. Muller, *The Global Reach,* p. 308).

The multinational corporations have even transformed the concept of industrialization. This can be seen from examples in many countries. For example, in the late nineteenth and early twentieth centuries some Latin American countries appeared to be industrializing on the strength of primary exports and a process of import substitution. Industrialization was initiated as domestic manufacturing, especially in non-durable consumer goods, was developed to capture the income derived from export earnings which had previously been spent on imported goods. Some countries experienced considerable growth on the basis of this import substitution. But there was an underlying weakness in economies remaining dependent on imported capital goods and remaining tied to the fortunes of primary exports. Such a pattern of growth could not easily be set by domestic considerations and an independent industrialization became even more difficult for such economies after the arrival of the multinational corporations. As more and more aspects of manufacturing fell into the hands of the U.S.-based multinationals, especially in the new industries, it became even less likely that technological development would reach a level that would permit the domestic production of capital goods. The U.S. corporations have no reason to create capital goods sectors in the countries where they operate. Thus even countries with successful primary export sectors find that the process of import substitution results in more foreign control, and "industrialization" means the parasitic growth of branch plants which are often little more than assembly plants and warehouse operations. (On this see Osvaldo Sunkel, "The Pattern of Latin American Dependence.")

Finally, the multinational corporations have even created the possibility of "de-industrialization." This point has been made by Professor James Laxer who has argued that the result of U.S. investment in some sectors of the Canadian economy, in particular in the automobile industry, has been the running down of Canadian industrial potential as the U.S. corporations have transferred production out of Canada into the United States in response to pressures there. (See J. Laxer, "Manufacturing in the Canadian Economy.")

*Domination as Internationalism*

The development of capitalism into a new phase of imperialism in the late ninteenth century had led both to world war and to civil wars in some countries. In fact, World War I had produced two profound changes. One was the emergence of the United States as the main contender for imperial supremacy, an event symbolized by her triumphant entry into the war in order to sort things out "over there." Secondly, as Elie Halevy pointed out long ago, "the world crisis was not only a war – the war of 1914 – but a revolution – the revolution of 1917" (*The World Crisis of 1914–18,* p. 5).

The carnage of World War I had produced the collapse of several European governments. In Russia the result was the revolutions of 1917 and the creation of the USSR. This event (like the revolution in China which resulted from a further round of imperialist rivalries) transformed the nature of the world economic system. Whatever else can be said about the Soviet Union, and however tragic was the later development of the revolution, it should not be forgotten that the economic development of the USSR provided a profound challenge to the capitalist world. The economic progress of the USSR which followed its break with capitalism was noted throughout the colonial world. Here was an example of a poor, illiterate, rural society rapidly reaching a position where, despite the bitter opposition of the capitalist powers from the very beginning, it could withstand first the invasion of Germany and later the encirclement of the United States.

The war had also done considerable damage to the prestige of liberalism, not least in non-European countries. A symbolic example of this was the Chinese intellectual Yen Fu, a believer in modernization and the translator of Herbert Spencer, T.H. Huxley, J.S. Mill, Montesquieu, and Adam Smith. (Edgar Snow relates, in *Red Star over China*, that these translations were read by the young Mao Tse-Tung.) After the war, the disillusioned Yen Fu thought that 300 years of European "progress" had brought only "profit self and kill others, diminish incorruptibility and banish shame" (quoted in John Dunn, *Modern Revolutions,* p. 78).

The rejection of political liberalism by many former adherents followed the general late-nineteenth century rejection of economic liberalism. The upsurge of national rivalries had reinforced the view, expressed early in that century in Germany and America, that free trade was something the British were trying to export along with their manufactured goods, to the detriment of industrially less developed nations. It was observed in other countries that protection had not been discarded by Britain until British capitalism had achieved supremacy in world markets. By the twentieth-century, even in Britain, the opinion began to be expressed that free trade was not a reliable formula for prosperity.

This is the background to the policy of internationalism pursued by the United States, beginning tentatively after the First World War and clearly visible after the Second. The world would be divided. On one side were the areas open to international capital movements, investment, and trade. This area was later known as the "free world." On the other side were the closed economies. The coining of the term "third world" after 1945 indicated that there would be a struggle over the disposition of the former colonial areas.

In the years after World War I, the United States had sought to establish its position at the centre of the capitalist world. It had done sufficiently well out of the war that the United States had been transformed from a debtor to a creditor nation (see H. Magdoff, *The Age of Imperialism,* chap. 3). The economic instability of the 1920's and 1930's contributed to a further weakening of London's role as the central banker of the capitalist world. Washington did not, however, quickly replace London. When Woodrow Wilson became president, proposals for a central bank were finally adopted despite populist opposition. But the Federal Reserve System, instituted in 1914, was at first run according to domestic concerns and not according to the requirements of an international gold standard. For example, in the early 1920's the Federal Reserve policy of deflation exacerbated the imbalance of international payments by causing a gold drain to the United States from 1920 to 1924. (A large gold reserve had already been built up during World War I and a further drain to the States occurred from 1934 to 1938. On this see Roy Harrod, *The Dollar,* esp. chap. 2.)

This new international situation was catastrophic for international trade and capital movements. A situation of rivalry in which no power was clearly dominant prevented the establishment of even short-term stability. That the United States was establishing herself as an international power, however, can be seen from her new influence in European affairs despite its failure to join the League of Nations. (See W.A. Williams, "The Legend of Isolationism in the 1920's.")

The States had an interest in attempts to restore trade stability, since it had by this time become a major exporter of industrial goods. Following World War I the belligerents met in Washington, far from the blandishments of the League of Nations, to attempt a new division of interests and to attempt to stabilize rivalries. The major nations at the 1921/22 Washington Conference were the States, Japan, Great Britain, France, and Italy.[3]

The United States made a further attempt at international stability with the Briand-Kellogg Pact (or the Pact of Paris) of 1928. This was originally proposed by the French as a treaty between France and the United States but the latter widened it into a international undertaking to renounce war as an instrument of national policy. After signature by the Great Powers it was accepted by 65 states. The treaty did not renounce the right to make war in self-defence. Significantly, Great Britain made it clear that "self-defence" included the right to defend "certain regions of the world the welfare and integrity of which constitute a special and vital interest for our peace and safety." For the States "self-defence" included any action required to prevent an infringement of the Monroe Doctrine. (See E.H. Carr, *International Relations Between the Two World Wars, 1919–1939,* pp. 117–23.)

U.S. delegations also played a major role in the various attempts to solve the problem of German reparations; the Dawes Committee, the Young Committee, and the Lausanne Conference. In late 1923, following the French occupation of the Ruhr and the disastrous German inflation, an international committee was set up to reorganize German finances. The initiative came from U.S. Secretary of State Hughes and the chairman was the American General Dawes. (See *ibid.,* p. 59.) A new plan for German reparations was negotiated in 1929 by the committee of financial experts chaired by the American Owen Young. One of the consequences of the new plan was the creation of a Bank of International Settlements.

The Lausanne Conference in June 1932 was a final attempt to settle the German reparations problem. The agreement was irrelevant in view of the fact that, in January, Brüning, the German chancellor, had declared that Germany would no longer pay reparations (*ibid.,* p. 147). The meeting at Lausanne called for a World Economic Conference in London in June 1933. The United States played a leading role in this conference, though Roosevelt's government appeared to be split on the major issues and the conference failed to produce an agreement for a new system of financial stability. (The Gold Standard had been abandoned by Britain in September 1931 and by the States in April 1933.) In the Tripartite Agreement of 1936 the United States, Britain, and France undertook to abstain from deliberate, excessive depreciation of their exchange rates and to consult before inevitable depreciations.

The United States government had been groping towards the re-establishment of an international economy. In the nineteenth century an open world economy had been established under the influence of British expansion. Britain had played a leading role in establishing an international currency system based on gold and sterling. World War I had resulted in a "re-nationalization" of the world economy, and Britain was no longer able to co-ordinate an open world economy.

Within a decade the limited and precarious agreements of the interwar years were in pieces. World War II was the result. Following the war there was once again the need for new international arrangements. This time, however, the United States was clearly in a position of dominance and the tentative policies of the past were replaced by an aggressive assertion of U.S. interests. The British of course still hoped to increase their influence in some areas, as did the French, but neither country was in a strong position to do so.[4]

The United States, however, had obviously learned that divisions of interest lead to wars and the danger of revolutions. In any case it was now in a position to increase its influence in many areas from which it previously had been excluded, or from which Churchill and others still hoped to exclude it. Rather than attempting to achieve domination from a position of independent "isolationism" or overt conflict, the States would achieve domination through "partnership" and "co-operation." U.S. opponents of the League of Nations had worried that the League would restrict U.S. foreign policy. U.S. supporters of the United Nations and NATO realized that these organizations could restrict *opposition* to the U.S. policy. (Note: See W.A. Williams, "The Legend of Isolationism in the 1920's.")

Cordell Hull outlined the new American foreign policy: "There will no longer be need for spheres of influence, for alliances, for balances of power, or any other of the special arrangements through which, in the unhappy past, the nations strove to safeguard their security or promote their interest." (See "Basis of the Foreign Policy of the United States," *Department of State Bulletin,* 25 March 1944, p. 276). Discriminatory trading systems, such as empire preference, were widely cited as a cause of political hostility and war. (See R. Gardner, *Sterling-Dollar Diplomacy,* pp. 9 and 19.) The United Nations Charter did, however, contain a provision, in Article 51, for regional security arrangements to take account of "Pan Americanism" and British Commonwealth interests, and the United States did not in fact relinquish control over its existing spheres of influence. The U.S. government made it clear to Britain, for example, that it regarded Latin America as a special U.S. preserve.[5]

U.S. leadership of a crusade for free trade appeared as part of the policy of internationalism. The movement for free trade, which did not always recognize the legitimacy of the complaints of others about U.S. barriers, had begun to develop in the States as that country rose to economic primacy.

One of the leading early proponents had been Woodrow Wilson. Wilson, like some nineteenth-century British liberals, had argued that free trade and world peace were one and indivisible. Wilson did not, however, assume that peace was easily imposed by means of liberal rhetoric. He took it for granted that the United States was involved in a struggle for overseas markets which alone could soak up surpluses, markets "to which diplomacy, and if need be power, must make an open way." Neither did he make the mistake of some liberals in assuming that "free-trade liberalism" was synonymous with "laissez-faire." "The Government," he said, "must open these gates of trade, and open them wide; open them before it is altogether profitable to open them, or altogether reasonable to ask private capital to open them at a venture" (quoted by W.A. Williams, *History as a Way of Learning,* p. 48).[6]

The Roosevelt administration began the process of reducing barriers to U.S. exports with the 1934 Reciprocal Trade Agreement and the negotiation of "most-favoured nation" agreements with a large number of countries. In the 1930's, however, there were not even many economists who were prepared to argue for free trade. Tariffs were widely seen as necessary protective measures. (See J.M. Keynes, *Means to Prosperity,* 1933.)

During World War II the American government renewed the pressure for changes. The British economic system was seen as one of the major targets. As a result of the leverage the Americans gained through the Lend-Lease Program they began to press Britain to change its policies. Rather than having supplies repaid in cash, the United States declared itself willing to receive payment in the form of acceptance by the British government of principles of policy favoured by the United States. U.S. Secretary of State Cordell Hull suggested that the policy he had in mind was liberalization of international trade. The United States wanted Britain to dismantle trade restrictions and discriminations (see Roy Harrod, *The Dollar,* pp. 93–116).

The U.S. government hoped to internationalize its policy of reducing barriers to trade through the creation of an International Trade Organization (ITO). The elimination of the Imperial Preference system was seen as a *sine qua non* of ITO. Prior to negotiations in Geneva in 1947, Will Clayton, U.S. Assistant Secretary of State, outlined the American strategy. Marshall aid would give the United States leverage to destroy the sterling bloc: "If we cannot now obtain the liquidation of the Ottawa system, we shall never do so. What we must have is a front-page headline that says "Empire Preference System Broken at Geneva". In fact the United States could not get its way because the British economy was too weak to sustain full "co-operation." (Clayton is quoted in G. and J. Kolko, *Limits of Power,* p. 366.)[7]

It was intended that ITO would be an outgrowth of the 1947 General Agreement on Tariffs and Trade (GATT). When the plans for ITO finally broke down in 1949, the essentials of the policy were in fact maintained through GATT's "most-favoured nation" clause which in principle prevents trade discrimination. GATT also prescribed that if protection was found to be necessary it should be achieved through a general tariff policy rather than through direct controls or restrictions.

American economic policy did not of course depend entirely on hopes for free trade agreements. An attempt had to be made to create conditions of economic stability in other countries. Without economic progress it was obvious that the "free enterprise" system itself was vulnerable. The need for a postwar system of international stability had been recognized even before the entry of the United States into the war. In late 1939 *Fortune* magazine organized a discussion among leading business men. They concluded: "What interests us primarily is the longer range question of whether the American capitalist system could continue to function if most of Europe and Asia should abolish free enterprise." The next peace settlement would have "to organize the economic resources of the world so as to make possible a return to the system of free enterprise in every country" (quoted in W.A. Williams, *The Tragedy of American Diplomacy,* p. 197). One thing that was obviously necessary was a new international monetary system. By 1944, the date of the establishment of the International Monetary Fund (IMF), the United States was sufficiently strong to impose its rules on the world and establish the dollar as the main reserve currency. Its imperial strength has been greatly enhanced by the role of the dollar as a reserve asset, since this has ensured that other countries carry part of the burden of defending the U.S. empire. (See G. Kolko, *The Politics of War,* esp. pp. 255–57 and Lukin Robinson, "The Downfall of the Dollar."

From the American viewpoint, the purpose of a sound international monetary system was to allow the United States to export goods and capital abroad in order to secure the sources of raw materials. The State Department director of the Office of Wartime Economic Affairs, Charles Taft, explained the problem in 1944: "Our metals are running out, and so may our oil eventually. ... Other essentials must come from abroad, and in 50 years, like the British, we shall have to export to pay for the things we need for life" (quoted in Kolko, *The Politics of War,* p. 254). In establishing a new monetary system the United States had to defeat the British proposal made by Keynes. Keynes' international system would have allowed countries with balance of payment problems to draw on a large overdraft allotment that would be controlled by nations in accordance with the prewar trading size. The U.S. plan, put forward by Harry Dexter White, emphasized the virtues of domestic restraint to maintain international balances, opposed exchange controls, associated loans with the ability of countries to export, promoted the role of the U.S. dollar as the main reserve currency to deal with short-term fluctuations, and allotted control of the IMF on the basis of reserves.

Keynes saw that Britain would have to yield. He wrote to the Chancellor of the Exchequer concerning the Bank of England's initial opposition to the IMF proposals: "The Bank of England do not allow for the fact that our postwar domestic policies are impossible without further American assistance. They do not allow for the fact that the Americans are strong enough to offer inducements to many or most of our friends to walk out on us, if we ostentatiously set out to start up an independent shop." (Quoted by D.E. Moggridge, *Keynes,* p. 37.)

The White plan was of course more favourable to the United States. In the past the British and the Americans had had to send their own bankers to other countries to establish central banking systems that were advantageous to foreign investors, as for example, had happened in the 1920's in Latin America (see C. Furtado, *Economic Development of Latin America,* chap. 9) and in Canada in the 1920's where the British played a major role in the new Bank of Canada. Now an international agreement would do the work for them, though they would continue to send IMF officials to supervise other countries. The rules of the IMF, as set up at Bretton Woods, were close to the U.S. proposal, thus allowing the Americans to "internationalize" their influence in other countries.

An underlying reality of "free enterprise" was the system of military alliances set up by the United States. The Marshall Plan, and other "foreign aid" schemes were extensions of the military alliances intended to open the world to the expansion of U.S. foreign investments which had become the key to the prosperity of American capitalism at home.

The definition of "freedom" had earlier been revealed by U.S. Secretary of State James Byrnes in July 1945: "What we must do now, is not to make the world safe for democracy, but make the world safe for the United States" (quoted by W.A. Williams, in "The American Century," p. 220). This strategy was clearly articulated in the Truman Doctrine of 1947. The Truman policy meant the division of the world into two: on the one hand, the "free world," that part of the world that was open to U.S. trade and investment, and, on the other hand, the "communist world," perceived as a monolithic bloc closed to U.S. capital. America's task was to maintain, and if possible enlarge, the "free world": "It must be the policy of the U.S. to support free peoples who are resisting subjugation by armed minorities or by outside pressure." (See D.F. Fleming, *The Cold War and Its Origins, 1917-1960.* Also G. Kolko, *The Roots of American Foreign Policy.*) Dean Acheson put this unselfish policy in a nutshell: "We are willing to help people who believe the way we do, to continue to live the way they want to live" (quoted in Williams, *History as a Way of Learning,* p. 6).

As General Marshall realized, it would be necessary to help others to think along the right lines: "It is idle to think that a Europe left to its own efforts would remain open to American business in the same way that we have known it in the past" (G. and J. Kolko, *The Limits of Power,* p. 376). The Marshall Plan was contingent upon agreement to an overall plan for European "co-operation" through the Committee for European Economic Co-operation. The United States also made sure of co-operation through the notorious "counterpart clause." This clause required recipients of U.S. aid to establish a fund in their own currency, equivalent to the sum received in U.S. dollars. The U.S. would own 5 per cent, the remaining 95 per cent could be used by the recipient only with U.S. approval.[8]

Thus in the years following World War II the United States emerged as a superpower. The international economy, that is, that part of it which was run along capitalist lines, was dominated by the United States. Economically and militarily the United States wielded power that would have been unthinkable a generation before. As a result of this the world entered upon a period of about twenty years in which American institutions and American ideas had an extraordinary influence in a large number of countries.

*Consequences*

In many parts of the world it has become obvious that imperial trading patterns block economic and social development and much of the political instability in the twentieth century must be seen against this background. The basic fact is that imperialism has brought only poverty and underdevelopment for millions of people. Imperialism has generally produced only barriers to economic development. The typical characteristics of the so-called "third world" countries are *not* those of the immature stages of the now developed capitalist societies. They are *not* characteristics of countries advancing towards industrialization. These countries are not so much characterized by a failure to develop, as by a distorted development, that is, an economic structure created in the interests of the imperialist power. (See André Gunder Frank, *The Sociology of Underdevelopment*.)

The imperial powers have had to contend with the growing threat to their world position, as people in their empires have realized that a new type of economic organization was necessary to obtain the freedom to recover their humanity and to achieve the freedom necessary to overcome poverty and disease. It has become obvious to anyone who cares to see that in many countries capitalist development has been both destructive and precarious because decisions concerning production are not made in the interest of the population of the region or country. The decisions are made in the headquarters of large corporations and on the basis of profitability to the owners of capital.

Some economists and politicians have called for more aid to promote development and perhaps avert the danger of revolution. Of course the horrors of poverty are real and the richer countries should help to end that poverty. But it will not be ended by the kind of campaign which aims at developing a feeling of guilt on the part of those who are not starving, while refusing to draw the conclusion that the poverty of the poor countries is perpetuated by their economic organization and frequently their subordinate relationship to imperial powers. Recently there has been a trend to replace "aid" with "trade." The problem is that trade also can create dependency. While it cannot be said that all trade promotes underdevelopment, the characteristic of international trade dominated by imperialist countries is to create a network of metropolis-hinterland relations.

The root of the problem lies in the fact that capitalism does not promote the trade which is a simple exchange of commodities. International trade is often presented as a mutually beneficial exchange of the surplus commodities of one country for the surplus commodities of another. But capitalist economies do not work that way. International exchanges among capitalist countries are overwhelmingly the result of the attempts by private interests in dominant countries to control the raw materials of other countries and to gain control of their markets. Nowadays the private interests are organized in giant corporations, and now, as in the past, the attempt to control raw materials and markets requires the resort to government influence. Giant U.S. corporations, for example, need the backing of the U.S. government in order to persuade foreign governments to allow them to control resources and markets. Even the largest corporations can only operate in countries that recognize and enforce their ownership rights and the right of movement of goods and capital.

Given the degree of concentration of capital that has been reached in the twentieth century, more and more corporations are forced to expand into foreign areas in order to re-invest capital more profitably than can be done at home. The consequence is that policies of free trade and capital movements can not result in "international" development. They can only allow free rein to the expansion of the corporations, which brings in its wake the problem of dependency and underdevelopment for the hinterland economies.

To the industrialists in imperialist countries it has always seemed natural that others should sell them food and minerals in exchange for manufactured goods. In the last century, Richard Cobden, the English parliamentarian who believed that world peace could be created through world trade, told the Italians "The sun is your coal."[9] He was not referring to solar energy. Today, many countries are subjected to the degradation that often results when the sun becomes their coal and tourism becomes the major economic activity.

The consequences of corporate trade and unhindered capital flows are underlined by the continuation of dependency throughout the world despite the ending of formal colonial relations in many countries since the 1950's. The maps of the 1970's may have more colours than the maps of the earlier part of the century, there may be more flags at the United Nations, but the reality of imperialist power remains. "Neocolonialism" shows that it may make little difference who occupies the governor's mansion. What counts is the control of the resources and the labour of the country. Dependency is not the result of a lack of economic activity. It is the result of economic activity controlled by foreign corporations for their own purposes. Dependency is not the result of a lack of resources necessary for economic survival in the twentieth century. It is the result of the unbalanced export of those resources as primary products. In many countries the export of these resources leaves only poverty, and many very poor countries actually export large quantities of foodstuffs to the imperialist world. (See Pierre Jalée, *The Pillage of the Third World.*)[10]

Dependency does not, however, always create poverty and the kind of underdevelopment associated with the "third world." The pattern of dependent development varies according to circumstance. Yet in all dependent countries, the unbalanced export of resources leads to distorted development and perpetuates dependency. The nature of dependency is shown in many countries by the continuation, after "formal" independence, of trade patterns established under colonial arrangements. One of the few major economic changes to result from the decolonization of the 1950's was the entry of the United States into areas previously barred to it. (This in fact was the aim of U.S. policy with regard to colonialism. See G. Kolko, *The Politics of War,* chap. 11.)

The political economy of imperialism continues to present a challenge to all subordinate nations. In some cases this is a matter of life and death. In others, the challenge, frequently "the American challenge," is more subtle as national sovereignty and cultures are slowly whittled away by economic take-overs and political compromises.

## Notes

**1.** For a discussion of the American Civil War as a "revolutionary offensive on the part of urban or bourgeois capitalist democracy," see Barrington Moore, *Social Origins of Dictatorship and Democracy,* p. 112. On the general analysis of southern society, see the studies by E. Genovese, in particular *The Political Economy of Slavery, The World the Slaveholders Made,* and "Marxian Interpretations of the Slave South." Despite the brilliance of his work, Genovese has considerable difficulty in classifying the American south, partly, it seems to me, because he underestimates its dependent relation to the industrial capitalist society of Britain.

**2.** For what it is worth, one study showed that in 1967 all but three of twenty-five large U.S.-controlled enterprises with subsidiaries in Britain were hedged against sterling devaluation. (See Raymond Vernon, *Sovereignty at Bay,* p. 167.) It is possible that it was ITT which started the run on sterling in 1972 that ended in the floating of the pound. (See A. Sampson, *The Sovereign State of ITT,* p. 107.) Such behaviour is hardly surprising. The executives of the multinational company are not disembodied world citizens but a group of men acting in the interests of their shareholders. A former employee of Shell Oil emphasizes the "Americanism" of the U.S. oil companies. Although many of their subsidiaries have a management consisting mainly of nationals of the country concerned, there are "key" U.S. personnel who ensure that "the policy of the subsidiary is in line with the authorized interpretation of centrally taken decisions" (Peter R. Odell, *Oil and World Power,* p. 4).

**3.** The conference is famous for its assigning of permissible battleship strength to the various powers, but there were also agreements on spheres of influence in the Pacific and an Open Door policy in China. Even British foreign policy was susceptible to U.S. pressure, as was shown by Britain's abandonment of its alliance with Japan in the face of American demands. (See M. Howard, *The Continental Commitment,* p. 88.) Harold Innis (in "Great Britain, The United States and Canada") stated that Arthur Meighen persuaded Britain to renounce the Anglo-Japanese alliance. Meighen's role is also discussed in R. Craig Brown and Ramsay Cook, *Canada 1896–1921,* pp. 292–93.

**4.** By 1940 it was apparent to the British government that it would have to seek economic, financial, and perhaps military support from the United States. Churchill welcomed what he called the "mixing-up" of some of the affairs of those "two great organizations of the English-speaking democracies, the British Empire and the United States" (quoted in J.B. Brebner *The North Atlantic Triangle,* p. 332). In fact it has been suggested by some historians that perhaps Churchill's greatest achievement was his clear recognition that Britain was dependent on the United States. (See, e.g., M. Howard, pp. 146–47.) As a result, Britain became one of the many countries that was encouraged to think that it had a special relationship with the United States. One of the implications of the "mixing-up" was the acknowledgement that Canada was in the U.S. sphere of influence.

**5.** See G. Kolko, *The Politics of War,* chap. 11. In May 1946 Eisenhower made this clear to all when he told the U.S. Congress that it was necessary to begin "securing within vital areas of S. America a structure that is oriented towards us militarily" (G. and J. Kolko, *The Limits of Power,* p. 79). With regard to Latin America the United States had long been accustomed to disguising its interests there as "internationalism." The United States had opposed schemes to create any kind of Latin American bloc in the name of "hemispheric co-operation," its own version of pan-Americanism. In general U.S. relations with Latin America provide a good guide to the significance of U.S. internationalism. In 1947, the Rio de Janeiro Treaty of Reciprocal Assistance set up what amounted to a permanent military treaty which subordinated Latin American countries to U.S. interests. Among other things, controversies were to be discussed in the inter-American system before being brought to the United Nations. In 1948 at Bogota, the treaty was systematized in the Organization of American States. (See Alonso Aguilar, *Pan-Americanism: From Monroe to the Present.*) The process of excluding Britain from South America had been underway for a long time. At the beginning of the century there were complaints from British interests in Colombia about "that economic penetration which is thought in the United States to be the proper accompaniment of the Monroe Doctrine" (quoted in V.G. Kiernan, "Imperialism, American and European," p. 123).

6. When Wilson visited Britain as part of his messianic tour of Europe in late 1918, he made two pilgrimages. One was to the church that had been attended by his mother's family. The other was to Free Trade Hall, Manchester, the symbolic home of nineteenth-century English liberalism. But Wilson's support of the international banking consortium and the repeal of the anti-trust laws for export associations show that he recognized that the twentieth century had brought changes in economic organization.

7. The Imperial Preference system had been set up at the Ottawa conference in 1932, though following the agreement, Britain, Canada, and Australia had all concluded trade agreements with other countries. The British government was perhaps more interested in commodity control arrangements than in tariffs, hoping to use price maintenance to ensure production and markets for British goods, plus financial security for shareholders and financial institutions. (See Ian M. Drummond, *British Economic Policy and the Empire, 1919–39,* chap. 3.) The empire was, however, of great importance to the British economy. From 1913 to 1938 the proportion of U.K. exports going to the empire rose from 22 per cent to 47 per cent, partially as a result of competition and tariffs in non-empire countries, and partially as a result of economic expansion in some parts of the empire (Drummond, *ibid.,* p. 18). In Canada British imports still enjoyed a tariff advantage over U.S. imports. The National Policy tariff had been set at 30 per cent on manufactured goods and 25 per cent on machinery. British goods paid on average 19.4 per cent, while U.S. goods paid on average 14.9 per cent. The first preferential system for British goods had been established by the Fielding Tariff of 1897. Canada's 1935 agreement with the U.S. reduced, but did not eliminate, the British advantages from the Ottawa agreements. (See O.J. McDiarmid, *Commercial Policy in the Canadian Economy.*)

At the Geneva meetings the United States offered a 50 per cent reduction on a wide range of imports, and Britain offered some reductions in preferences. It was believed that the U.S. government had in fact threatened withdrawal of aid. At the same time the States was still creating its own empire system, concluding in 1946 a preferential tariff system with the Phillipines similar to that which already existed with Cuba.

ITO was actually defeated in the end by opposition from sections of the U.S. business community who believed that quantitative restrictions could be continued. They also objected to the inclusion of a statement that the United States had a responsibility for international full employment. Such a statement might lead, they thought, to a planned economy. (See G. and J. Kolko, *The Limits of Power,* chap. 23 and R. Gardner, *Sterling-Dollar Diplomacy,* chap. 17.)

**8.** Even labour "internationalism" became part of American policy. (On this see R. Radosh, *American Labour and United States Foreign Policy.*) The U.S. government had discovered at the time of World War I that it could use some labour leaders to promote its foreign policy. The AFL had decided to stay out of the International Federation of Trade Unions that was set up in Amsterdam in 1919, entering only in the late 1930's. But towards the end of World War II in 1944, the AFL endorsed the creation of the Free Trade Union Committee (FTUC), which became an instrument of U.S. Cold War policy.

In France, for example, the FTUC worked closely with the State Department and also received funds from the CIA. A former official of the CIA explained later that money had been used to: "pay off strong-arm squads in Mediterranean ports, so that American supplies could be unloaded against the opposition of communist dock workers. In [1949] the communist CGT led a strike in Paris which came near to paralyzing the French economy. A take-over of the government was feared. Into this crisis stepped Lovestone and his assistant Irving Brown (of the FTUC). With funds from Dubinsky's union, they organized *Force Ouvrière* a non-Communist union. When they ran out of money they appealed to the CIA. Thus began the secret subsidy of free trade unions. ..." (Quoted by Radosh, p. 323.) Following the accession to leadership of Walter Reuther in 1946, and the purge of unions under communist influence, the CIO joined the AFL in supporting Cold War policies (*ibid.*, pp. 436-37).

The AFL-CIO left the International Confederation of Free Trade Unions in 1969.

In Canada, the policy was exemplified in the emergence of the SIU, backed by U.S. unions and the U.S. government with the tolerance of the Canadian government against the wishes of the Canadian trade union movement. (See R.M. Laxer, *Canada's Unions*, chap. 12.) In another case, the U.S. trade unions took control of, against the wishes of Canadian trade unionists, a United Textile Workers of America strike. The leadership of the Canadian union was simply dismissed and a strike settled by American representatives. (See Laxer, chap. 17.)

**9.** Cobden is quoted in E.J. Hobsbawm, *The Age of Revolution*, p. 216. As it happens, northern Italy did develop under capitalism, though the path was extremely uneven, leading through both imperialism in Africa and fascism. Furthermore, the development of the north occurred at the expense of the south. But even in the 1950's, Enrico Mattei, the director of the state-owned oil and gas industry, found it difficult to protect Italian development against the new "free-traders," the U.S. oil interests who opposed him at every turn until he died in an air crash. (On Mattei and more general questions, see M. Tanzer, *The Political Economy of International Oil and the Underdeveloped Countries*.)

**10.** The difficulties of the interwar years, especially the depression of the 1930's, led to a renewed interest in long-term economic growth and a search for new theories. The challenge of non-capitalist systems of industrialization had spread shock waves around the colonial world, and of course around the centres that controlled the colonial world. Keynesian theory was developed into growth theory by Harrod and Domar and the battle for the "third world" was on.

But even in the new "development" theory, the market assumptions retained a dominant place. Of course not all economists accepted the orthodox view. In fact as Simon Kuznets put it in 1955 in his *Toward a Theory of Economic Growth* (p. 3): "The recent emphasis on the problem of economic growth stems from the realization that the 19th-century theory of the international division of labour, with its promise of the inevitable and rapid spread of modern economic civilization to all corners of the earth, is hardly tenable." Not only had some countries failed to "develop," but as some economists recognized by this time, the "international division of labour" had actually *created* something which could be called *underdevelopment.* This point was made by Celso Furtado in *Development and Under-development, 1961*: "Underdevelopment is a discrete historical process through which economies that have already achieved a high level of development have not necessarily passed." Furtado went further. Underdevelopment, he argued, is "a special process due to the penetration of modern capitalistic enterprises into archaic structures." This is not necessarily the precise cause of the problem but it is clear that economic development has to be considered not merely with reference to the extension of the market and the division of labour but to the particular international framework within which extension of the market occurs.

# FOUR
# The Political and Economic Framework of Development

Canada was profoundly affected by the history of the United States. In the first half of the twentieth century the balance of power in the North Atlantic Triangle had changed dramatically. The British corner of the triangle was quickly reduced as a source of power and even as a point of reference in Canadian life, while the growth of American corporations and the policies of the U.S. government, particularly those developed during and after World War II, led to a pervasive U.S. presence in Canada.

The extent of U.S. economic control in Canada reached a level that made Canada unique among industrial nations. By the mid-1960's foreign-owned corporations, primarily from the United States, accounted for more than 60 per cent of the manufacturing sector, of the mining and smelting sector, and of the petroleum and natural gas sectors of the Canadian economy. In some important industries, such as automobiles and rubber, U.S. control was close to 100 per cent, and it was about 80 per cent in chemicals and electrical apparatus. Payments of interest and dividends to foreigners were running at more than a billion dollars per year, while payments for business services, which include management fees, royalties, franchises, advertising, and professional services, was about $245 million per year. This latter figure in particular was indicative of a change in the nature of foreign investment in Canada. In 1945 about 40 per cent of all foreign long-term investment was *direct* investment. By the mid-1960's this figure had grown to 60 per cent.

About 80 per cent of this foreign direct investment came from the United States. These figures meant that a huge portion of the Canadian economy had come under the control of large, U.S.-based corporations. (These figures are taken from the Report of the Task Force on the Structure of Canadian Industry, *Foreign Ownership and the Structure of Canadian Industry.* The chairman of the Task Force was Professor M.H. Watkins.)

Such a situation obviously invited a reaction. The Toronto *Globe and Mail* attempted to summarize one point of view by presenting what it saw as the realistic view of events: "It is probable that we have already advanced too far along the road to economic union with the United States for turning back to be possible. They need our resources, we want their standard of living" (*Globe and Mail,* 31 December, 1965, quoted in Walter L. Gordon, *A Choice for Canada,* p. x). The *Globe* went on to say that in the first place little could be done since the United States could take the resources by force if necessary. Inevitably we had lost economic control and a certain measure of political control, but in any case "geography weds us, language weds us, culture weds us." The *Globe and Mail* was certainly right in perceiving that what had happened had not been merely a "take-over" of the Canadian economy, but also the assimilation of Canadian government policies to U.S. interests. It was in fact the acceptance of U.S. "internationalism" in all its manifestations that quickly reduced Canadian sovereignty and "wedded" Canada to its neighbour – geographically, linguistically, and culturally.

### *Liberal Continentalism*

As was noted in chapter 2, the Ogdensburg Agreement had been a political turning point. During World War II a series of developments brought the Canadian government closer to the United States and prepared Canada for acceptance of postwar "internationalism."

The outbreak of war in Europe presented particular difficulties for the Canadian government. It was obvious that British involvement would automatically raise the question of Canada's role, and that domestic conflicts over the use of the Canadian army would once again appear. It seems that, from Munich on at least, Mackenzie King assumed that Canada would support Britain, though there were influential Liberals, such as O.D. Skelton, the under-secretary of state for external affairs, who favoured neutrality. (See J.L. Granatstein, *Canada's War: The Politics of the Mackenzie King Government, 1939–1945.*) King took a large view of events in Europe, seeing that war raised many political problems. After the invasion of Poland he wrote in his diary: "Heaven knows whether socialist aims at world revolution may not manifest themselves all over the world" (Granatstein, p. 13). The Canadian prime minister was in fact in a dilemma because he believed that German victory would mean the triumph of force and materialism over the reason and spiritualism of England and France, but a German defeat would mean control of Europe by the communists (*ibid.*, p. 27).

Canada's approach to the United States was determined by two factors. One was the U.S. concern over the consequences of a possible British defeat in 1940, following the collapse of France. The other was the economic dislocation of industry caused by the war.

Some influential figures in the United States began planning for hemispheric economic co-ordination. A.A. Berle, the U.S. assistant secretary of state, discussed this concept with Hugh Keenleyside, first secretary in the Department of External Affairs, who had been sent to Washington by King. (These events are discussed in R.D. Cuff and J.L. Granatstein, *Canadian-American Relations in Wartime,* chap. 5, and in J.L. Granatstein, *Canada's War,* esp. pp. 145-47). Keenleyside participated in studies for co-ordinating war production, but also, it appears, speculated further about the implications. Berle noted in his diary that: "Keenleyside realizes this is now one continent and one economy; that we shall have to be integrated as to finance, trade routes, and pretty much everything else; and in this I so thoroughly agree with him that it is refreshing. We talked long and happily about it – though much lies in the realm of dreams." (J.L. Granatstein, p. 146)[1]

The Permanent Joint Board of Defence and then, in June 1941, a Joint Economic Committee were created within the framework of hemispheric planning. This hemispheric view became global after the bombing of Pearl Harbor, and Canada's role in U.S. policy was correspondingly subordinated in importance, but mobilization for war had a permanent effect on the Canadian economy.

At the opening of World War II Canada's economic policy was based on a bilateral imbalance within a balanced North Atlantic triangle. A Canadian trade deficit with the United States was balanced by a surplus with the United Kingdom. (See R.S. Sayers, *U.K. Financial Policy,* pp. 322-23. See also Cuff and Granatstein, chap. 4). An imbalance in the whole was threatened as the British economy was re-organized for war. In particular it seemed probable that, following the Lend-Lease arrangement, Britain would switch from Canada to the United States for war purchases, producing indirectly a problem for Canada's balance of trade with the United States. The Canadian government was unwilling to control imports from the United States or to freeze dividend payments from Canada to that country, actions which would antagonize U.S. interests and especially grieve Cordell Hull, one of Canada's "champions" in Washington (Cuff and Granatstein, p. 77). The trade imbalance was rendered more delicate by the possibility that some Americans would push for the liquidation of U.S. assets held by Canadians, just as they had done with regard to British assets in the U.S. The solution was the Hyde Park Declaration of April 1941 which co-ordinated U.S. and Canadian defence production, guaranteed the access of the United States to Canadian war materials, and allowed for British acquisitions under Lend Lease to be sent to Canada for further production.

The war had obviously created special conditions which required a government response. Yet King and his government entered into extraordinary negotiations with the United States, often in a completely informal way. King apparently saw the rise of the U.S. empire in the western hemisphere, and he was concerned about the U.S. presence in the far north. (See J.L. Granatstein, p. 321.) There were other Liberals who also noted the trend. In 1944 W.A. Mackintosh wrote to a friend that "In economic as well as in political thinking the United States is veering towards imperialism" (*ibid.,* p. 323). Yet King continued to seek political popularity by claiming a special relationship with Roosevelt and throughout the war years contrived to have himself photographed in the role of influential mediator. (See Donald Creighton, *Canada's First Century,* esp. the photograph facing p. 288.)

The consequences of Canadian military integration with the United States were spelled out in 1944 by the chairman of the Canadian Joint Staff Mission in Washington. General Pope saw that the United States would wish to continue the alliance:

> To the Americans the defence of the United States is continental defence, which includes us, and nothing that I can think of will ever drive that idea out of their heads. Should, then, the United States go to war with Russia they would look to us to make common cause with them and, as I judge their public opinion, they would brook no delay. ... [We should] ensure that there was no apprehension as to our security in the American public mind. As I used to hold ten years ago when I was in Operations, what we have to fear is more a lack of confidence in the United States as to our security, rather than enemy action. (Quoted in James Eayrs, *In Defence of Canada,* vol. 3, pp. 320–21.)

It is important to note that the United States had also used the period of World War II to further subordinate the Canadian *economy* to its own interests. The 1941 Hyde Park Agreement led to integration for war production and no termination date was set.[2] A note from the U.S. ambassador, dated 7 May, 1945, proposed an extension to cover the war with Japan and the period of reconversion, and stated that: "in no case should priorities assistance be given to a Canadian manufacturer to make civilian goods which are prohibited in this country by War Production Board Order." (See R.A. Mackay, *Canadian Foreign Policy, 1945–1954,* sec. III, A.)

In April 1949, that is, before the outbreak of the Korean War, the United States proposed the creation of a Joint Industrial Mobilization Committee, to be responsible for co-operation with the Permanent Joint Board of Defence on matters of industrial mobilization.

Canada's participation in a permanent military alliance, NATO, was sweetened by Lester Pearson's assertion that NATO was more than a military alliance against the Soviet Union. To make this possible, Article 2 of the NATO agreement, on social and economic collaboration, was inserted at Pearson's insistence, despite the fact that it was an annoyance to some Americans, including Dean Acheson. (See Cuff and Granatstein, chap. 6.) To the extent that NATO was concerned with social and economic collaboration it was directed at opposing the influence of communist parties in western Europe.

In 1953 the Joint Canada-U.S. Committee on Trade and Economic Affairs was set up. This was a committee at the ministerial level. In 1956, when questioned in the House about the frequency and agenda of meetings of this committee, the Minister of Trade and Commerce, Mr. C.D. Howe, replied that there was no fixed timetable. He went on: "There is no formal agenda prepared long in advance. We have an *ad hoc* agenda, but there is no great formality associated with these meetings. They usually last one evening and one day and they are carried on with considerable informality." See Mackay, p. 90.)

No doubt many Canadians took a "pragmatic" view of U.S. investment in Canada and U.S. continental policies. Perhaps they brought wealth, and on the whole Americans were seen as a benign influence in a troubled world. In 1956, however, the arrogance of the Liberals and concern over the proposed Trans-Canada Pipeline gave rise to a nationalist reaction sufficient to produce a political effect. The result was the election of the Diefenbaker government.

The election of Diefenbaker disrupted the smooth relations between Ottawa and Washington. The U.S. government saw Diefenbaker as a nuisance. In some cases it appears that U.S. subsidiaries in Canada intervened in an attempt to bring Canadian policies into line with U.S. wishes. Diefenbaker has stated that when the U.S. government was attempting to dissuade Canada from selling wheat to China in 1961, Imperial Oil threatened to withhold supplies of bunker fuel from ships carrying wheat to China. (See J.G. Diefenbaker, *One Canada,* vol. 2, p. 179.)

Following the wavering of some members of the Canadian government during the 1962 "Cuban missile crisis" and the 1963 Bomarc wrangle, the U.S. government let it be known that it no longer had confidence in Diefenbaker, and the U.S. view played a role in the re-election of a Liberal government. The political climate in Canada had changed, however, and even a Liberal government showed that it could bring in measures that were not to the liking of continentalists. (On the Diefenbaker period see Peter C. Newman, *Renegade in Power.*)

Liberal Finance Minister Walter Gordon's first budget, in June 1963, was a radical departure from his party's usual policies. Gordon proposed to introduce a take-over tax of 30 per cent on the sales of shares in Canadian companies to foreign individuals or corporations and he also proposed a new form of withholding tax on dividends paid outside the country. Gordon was immediately pilloried in the press by influential businessmen, and the proposals were withdrawn, but the issue of foreign ownership had been injected into Canadian politics. (See Peter C. Newman, *The Distemper of Our Times,* esp. pp. 13–26.)

In the second half of the 1960's opposition to foreign corporations in Canada grew markedly. An opinion poll showed that, by 1972, 47 per cent of Canadians thought that U.S. ownership of companies was bad for the Canadian economy, while only 38 per cent thought it was good. Some 22 per cent wanted more U.S. capital, but 67 per cent expressed the view that Canada had enough. (See John Fayerweather, *Foreign Investment in Canada,* New York, p. 14.) This shift in attitudes to foreign investment was accompanied by a strong current of opposition to other manifestations of the American presence in Canada, particularly in schools and universities, in the media and the arts and also in the trade union movement. Canadian opinion began to polarize and it did so in an interesting and significant way. A study by an American investigator showed that "elites" in Canada were more favourable to foreign investment than was the general population (see Fayerweather, chap. 2). This information is important in assessing the process by which the United States had become a dominant force in Canadian life.

Professor Donald Creighton has argued that a critical change occurred in the late 1930's. Since that time, he states, a series of Liberal governments led by Mackenzie King, Louis St. Laurent, and Lester Pearson shifted Canada from the British orbit and placed it firmly in the U.S. empire. Creighton points in particular to the role of King and his influential cabinet minister, C.D. Howe. Howe, the "economic continentalist" was King's "perfect associate." Together they readily complied in "the series of discreet, informal bargains which, since 1940, has been one of the most distinctive features of Canadian foreign policy." (See D. Creighton, *Towards the Discovery of Canada,* p. 169.)

There can be no doubt that the King-Howe years did witness significant changes, as we have already seen. Canadian trade was redirected to such an extent that by 1950 65 per cent of Canada's exports went to the United States. Between 1946 and 1957 foreign, mostly American, control of manufacturing increased from 35 per cent to 56 per cent, of mining and smelting from 38 per cent to 70 per cent. Howe abetted the take-over in various ways. Millions of dollars' worth of war plants were sold to foreign corporations at bargain prices. Among them were the Victory Aircraft plant at Malton, which was sold to British A.V. Roe, and the Canadair plant at Montreal, sold to U.S. General Dynamics. Branch plant expansion was also encouraged by extremely generous depreciation rates which allowed fast tax write-offs. (See M.H. Watkins, "Economic Development in Canada.")

These points notwithstanding, it is a misleading simplification to suggest that the Liberal government was the sole agent of continentalism. First, there were no clear differences between the political parties with regard to important aspects of continentalism during this period Liberals, Conservatives, and the CCF-NDP alike had accepted many of the assumptions of the U.S. government and had explicitly or implicitly allied themselves with U.S. expansion. It was St. Laurent and Pearson who had introduced the U.S. cold war rhetoric into Canada and who had tried to teach Canadians to think like Americans. (See St. Laurent's speech of June 11, 1948, in R. Mackay, p. 184, and Pearson's speech of Jan. 20, 1955, *ibid.*, p. 185.) But when the Conservatives returned to office in 1957 there was no noticeable change in most of the underlying assumptions of Canadian foreign policy. Both Diefenbaker and Secretary of State for External Affairs Howard Green, employed the same cold war concepts as were used by U.S. foreign policy spokesmen to justify their aggressive policies from the 1940's to the 1970's. Thus the Conservatives, too, invited Canadians to think like Americans. (See James Eayrs, *Northern Approaches,* pp. 149–50, for examples.)

Secondly, the mechanism of the American take-over has to be sought at a deeper level. The attitudes of political parties have been of major importance in the process of take-over, but these political attitudes have been the result not simply of the process of political organization, but of a larger process of social formation. This was made apparent by the failures of the one prime minister in recent Canadian history who did hold nationalist views and who promised to direct Canada towards a "new national policy."

The inability of John Diefenbaker to articulate an adequate Canadian economic policy frustrated his nationalist sentiments. As George Grant argued in *Lament for a Nation* (pp. 13–15), Diefenbaker's populism and "small-town free enterprise" economic philosophy were totally at odds with his rhetoric about Canadian sovereignty. Grant's conclusion was that, after 1940 at any rate, economic "nationalism had to go hand in hand with some measure of socialism," since only economic planning could "restrain the victory of continentalism." A "new national policy" required some element of economic planning, but policies of economic planning are at variance with the economic interest of the multinational corporations and are also at variance with the prevailing liberal doctrines of economic development. Both the presence of U.S.-based corporations and liberal economic theory have continentalist results in Canada and thus work against Canadian nationalism.

*The Creation of Dependency*

The economic take-over and its political and cultural consequences created what can be called a condition of dependency. Canada became a dependent country in the American empire. One could also say that Canada became a peripheral society in relation to the U.S. centre. Dependency resulted from a complex process of social change which was the result of the interaction of forces existing within both Canadian and American society.

In explaining this process we have to consider how a social structure is created by specific patterns of economic development and also how that social structure changes with shifts in the international economic framework. The social structure of a periphery country will be strongly influenced by the nature of the relationship between the periphery country and its particular centre country and will also be subjected to changes that are occurring in the centre country as well as in the periphery country itself.[3]

For geographic, economic, political, and social reasons, for each country at any given time, there is a particular system of integration in the world economy. This system is defined by the pattern of international trade in goods and services and of transactions on capital account. Dependent or periphery economies, like Canada, are brought into a world economy whose pattern is heavily influenced by dominant or centre economies. During most of the last century, for example, the international economy was basically shaped by the British economy.

However, the model of integration of a periphery country is not simply an adaptation to the overall world economic pattern. Since the method of integration differs for each of the centres, that of each periphery country will be determined by the particular centre within whose sphere of influence it is placed. Thus the Canadian

West was developed in the context of a late nineteenth-century Britain eager for food imports. The fact that British capital was available for investment in transportation was an added factor in linking Canada to the British economy.

Each particular system of centre-periphery relations, when once established, tends to exhibit considerable resistance to change but such systems do change. In every centre, in relations between the centres, and in the peripheries, changes which are more or less important are continuously taking place. These changes may be slow or they may be dramatic, as for example, when World War I seriously weakened the position of Britain as an exporter of capital.

Thus the periphery countries will be subjected to successive transformations to accommodate themselves to a new pattern of integration in the world economy as the centre economies change. Also, since each centre has its specific system of integrating peripheries, the periphery countries will be subjected to transformations to compensate for shifts in the relative weight and in the spheres of influence of the different centres. For example, both the nature of the economic development of the United States and the rise of U.S. economic power relative to that of Britain had a profound impact on the Canadian economy. What appeared in the 1920's as a change in the peripheral nature of the Canadian economy, that is as a development towards independence, was in fact a transition to a new peripheral relationship with a new centre.

This does not mean of course that events in the peripheral country are merely passive. International economic relations do not develop within a social vacuum. To each model of integration in the international economy, there corresponds a social structure in which the groups involved in specific economic activities establish themselves internally and externally. For example, in the last century, bankers and railway promoters had a dominant role in Canadian society. In this century railway promoters became less important than branch plant managers. This change was not merely the result of changes within Canada, but reflected Canada's changing relationship with Britain and the United States. Finally, it is obvious that government policies will be formulated with regard to changing conditions and the relative power of the groups attached to each system of integration with a centre economy.

A study of the political economy of Canada must take into

account both the changing social structure and the related changing international economic conditions. Much of the literature on foreign trade and economic development has failed to integrate the two and hence has been one-sided, stressing either the inevitability of development or the inevitability of underdevelopment, without explaining why the dependent countries of the world show such a great variety of standards of living and social structure.[4]

It is convenient to begin an analysis of Canada's dependency by considering the dominant social group within the country.

Canada's development has been strongly marked by the influence of a class of merchants and bankers, at first based primarily in Montreal, later based in Montreal and Toronto. This has been documented by many historians and some of our most prominent historians, particularly Harold Innis and Donald Creighton, have made this a major theme of study.

Harold Innis, for example saw the emergency of centralization of decision-making and the strengthening of paternalism in New France as a result of the need to establish monopoly in the fur trade in order to compete with the British. "Centralized control as shown in the activities of the government, the church, the seigniorial system, and other institutions, was in part a result of the overwhelming importance of the fur trade. ... The institutional development of New France was an indication of the relation between the fur trade and the mercantile policy." (*The Fur Trade*, p. 391)[5]

Innis also explained how the Canadian government has acted as an instrument of both the imperial country and the Canadian elite. In the days of the British Empire the Canadian state served as a guarantor of the loans of British investors and banking houses and at the same time served their partners, the Canadian merchants. Both the Act of Union of 1840 and Confederation were identified by Innis as instruments to secure low interest rates for the transportation system. Donald Creighton went even further. In discussing the British government's decision to support the proposals made at Quebec for confederation, he said: "This British assistance might be interpreted as an effort to assist in the creation of a great holding company in which could be amalgamated all those divided and vulnerable North American interests whose protection was a burden to the British state and whose financial weakness was a grievance of British capital" (*British North America at Confederation,* p. 10).

The historical analysis by Innis and Creighton has been extended by means of concepts drawn from the literature on the political economy of underdevelopment. (This analysis was introduced by Tom Naylor, "The Rise and Fall of the Third Commercial Empire of the St. Lawrence." See also Naylor's two-volume study, *The History of Canadian Business, 1867-1914.*)

Capitalism in Canada has created a mercantile class which has been able to accumulate wealth through the circulation of commodities, rather than through their production. The merchant class began its history in the days of the fur trade and then extended its economic interests into landholding, the timber trade, and the early wheat trade. They did expand into some processing industries, such as brewing and flour milling, but mostly when they expanded from mercantile activities they chose to move into financial activities rather than into industry. This mercantile and financial class decided that a primary economic role for the government should be to ensure that transportation networks and tariff policies were adequate to promote, and protect, trade routes in Canada and from Canada to overseas markets. The maintenance of trade, from which they drew their profits, was the main interest of the Canadian merchants and bankers.

Such a policy did not lead the merchants and financiers into conflict with the interests of the imperial country. The British economy, increasingly in need of raw materials, was able to supply portfolio capital for the development of the transportation systems. The Canadian bankers played an important intermediary role in the investment of British capital and thus consolidated their position in Canada.

The role of the mercantile and financial class became more problematic with the industrialization of the American economy. There were two main choices. The merchants and financiers could have decided to protect Canada from U.S. expansion by promoting an independent industrialization in Canada. Or they could have decided to perpetuate their role as an intermediary class in a centre-periphery economic relationship by continuing to solicit British investment in Canada and in addition by supporting the introduction of U.S. capital into Canada. Obviously the economic assumptions of Confederation and the National Policy would be critical in deciding which policy would be followed.

Professor Naylor has argued that the National Policy did not aim at providing a protected market for Canadian industrial capitalists. Rather it aimed at creating industry in Canada which would provide benefits for the merchant capitalists and bankers. Thus the attraction of foreign capital and branch plants was acceptable to them as a form of development. The ultimate result was that the Canadian economy remained dependent. Within Canada, the Montreal commercial community remained dominant as a result of the pattern of dependence and "the stultification of industrial entrepreneurship followed from their control of the state and state policy, most notably with regard to the structure of the federally controlled banking system. The resulting vacuum led directly to the reliance on American industrialism, in the form of entrepreneurs, patents, or direct investment." (Naylor, *The History of Canadian Business,* vol. 2, p. 283)

This argument depends heavily on an analysis of the Canadian banking system. The Canadian banks had as their primary function the financing of commodity movements rather than the provision of long-term capital. In addition the railwaymen, bankers, and land companies were in favour of rapid resource exploitation which has meant turning to foreign markets to maximize sales. The merchants and bankers were not overly concerned with the ownership of industry in Canada, so long as they could live off whatever industry there was.

As far as the interests of merchants and bankers are concerned the argument is convincing. Less certain, however, is the implication that the National Policy invited dependency. The tariff did encourage U.S. direct investment in Canada, and this point was certainly understood by the 1890's at least. (See O.J. McDiarmid, *Commercial Policy in the Canadian Economy.*) Naylor adds the argument that accompanying legislation on patents and municipal bonusing are further evidence that the National Policy did not encourage Canadian industry, but rather promoted foreign industry in Canada. (See *The History of Canadian Business,* vol. 2, esp. chaps. 11–13.)

Yet in the political debates concerning the National Policy it certainly appeared that the policy was seen as an alternative to continentalism. The policy had been so introduced by Macdonald. In the 1880's, the evidence of substantial opposition to the tariff, especially in rural western Ontario where farmers favoured the idea of commercial union with the United States, raised the question of what policies the Liberal Party would endorse. (See Robert Craig Brown, *Canada's National Policy, 1883-1900: A Study in Canadian-American Relations,* chap. 6.)

Laurier, the new leader of the Liberals, believed in free trade and by the 1891 election the Liberal Party stood for unrestricted reciprocity. One of the issues underlying the debate was whether reciprocity would lead to political union, though the subject was complicated by the fact that the Conservatives had left open the possibility of reciprocity with the United States if such an agreement could be negotiated. Washington, however, at this point was in the process of raising tariffs. The Liberals attempted to maintain a clear separation between commercial union and political union, though there appeared to be some uncertainty within their ranks. John Charlton, the Liberal Party emissary to Washington, who was sent there to offset Goldwin Smith's entreaties for reciprocity and political union, wrote in his diary:

> Goldwin Smith has been advising a declaration on the part of the United States that if we want reciprocity we must take it in connection with Political Union and we want to prevent that. Reciprocity is what we want, the declaration for Political Union would create a ferment, fire the tory heart, and solidify prejudices. We want free Commercial intercourse, Commercial Union in fact, and the Political Question may be left to take care of itself. The future will settle it and all we are called upon now to do is to secure a policy that will give material prosperity to Canada. (Quoted in R.C. Brown, pp. 244–45)

The Liberals began to modify their position of opposition to the National Policy when, following the 1891 election, former Liberal leader Edward Blake published his "West Durham letter" which argued that trade policy could not be separated from the question of the political future. By 1896 Laurier had given in to business pressure, and as prime minister at least tacitly supported the National Policy until 1911. (*Ibid.*, pp. 246 and 269. Premier Mowat of Ontario joined Blake in expressing reservations about trade liberalization.)

The National Policy was thus seen as a necessary adjunct to

nationalism even though the consequences were far from nationalist. Perhaps the reason must be sought in the nature of the multinational corporation. Prior to the 1880's foreign investment, even direct investment, did not have the same results that it was to have in the era of the multinational corporation. Before 1880 when American entrepreneurs such as Daniel Massey, Hiram Walker, or, even later, Francis Henry Clergue, came to Canada they established themselves as Canadian businessmen and owners of Canadian industries. But towards the end of the century foreign direct investment was a necessary outlet for American corporations, and thus led to the creation of branch plants, which were not Canadian industries, but American industry in Canada. By 1914, U.S. branch plants were about 10 per cent of total capital in Canada and they were predominant in the electrical and chemical industries and also those industries based on the internal combustion engine. These were the industries that brought about what some economic historians have called the "second industrial revolution." At the same time American corporations sought control of the new resources necessary to U.S. industrialization; the metals of the Canadian shield, pulp and paper from the Canadian forests, hydro-electric power from Canadian rivers. (See H.V. Nelles, *The Politics of Development: Forests, Mines, and Hydro-Electric Power in Ontario, 1894-1941,* esp. chap. 8.)

The Ontario government sought to direct the surge of American expansion. Hydro-electric power was brought under public control, but the attempt to impose a "manufacturing condition" on resource industries, to promote processing of resources in Canada, generally proved unworkable.[6] Canadian governments were prepared to modify their laissez-faire liberalism to a certain extent but not to the extent that would mean general opposition to foreign investment and market forces. "Public enterprise," tax and tariff policies, did not reverse the prevailing continentalist economic forces. As Professor Nelles puts it: "As early as the 1890's it had become apparent that Canadian objectives would not be met within the ordinary workings of the market system, or more particularly, within the boundaries laid down by American commercial policy" (*ibid.*, p. 308).

Once U.S. branch plants had established themselves in Canada their domination of industry precluded innovation and supported the continuation of a social structure that had allowed them to become dominant. And on the other side, the prevalence of U.S. investment tied the fortunes of the Canadian economy to its success. In 1919 the President of the Canadian Reconstruction Association, an organization through which the Canadian Manufacturers' Association repelled the farmers' attack on the tariff, explained that in their view a switch to a low-tariff policy would mean: "the prostration of industries, much unemployment, exodus of Canadians to American industrial centres, summary stoppage of the establishment of American factories in Canada and a great check to industrial and national development" (quoted in W.L. Morton, *The Progressive Party in Canada,* p. 76).

Canada had fallen into an economic position characterized by continued reliance on staple exports and the dominating presence of U.S. corporations. These multinational corporations acted as a continentalist force, and the tariff policy was totally inadequate in the face of such pressures.

There can be little doubt about the consequences of the National Policy. Canada had become a dependent country. This does not mean that the precise results of the National Policy were foreseen, or that merchants and bankers held a very far-sighted view of the consequences of their actions. Probably in most cases they adopted procedures that seemed to them most profitable in the immediate future. In the same way Canadian governments have mostly reacted to immediate pressures and have generally operated with a limited set of assumptions about the possibilities of economic development.

Yet the result was not entirely accidental. The limitations of the businessmen and politicians were not merely the consequence of a complacent optimism about the future, bolstered by a reassuring prosperity in the present. The range of acceptable policies was dictated by a powerful ideology which grew out of a well-established social structure. Overwhelmingly, government policies were framed within the limitations of private property and private capital investment, even if a degree of government support was necessary as a supplement.

Canada did develop a tradition of "public enterprise." (See the important study by Herschel Hardin, *A Nation Unaware.*) Public investment in transportation, in communications, in hydro-electric power, and in atomic energy has reduced foreign control in these sectors of the economy. In addition, legislation has maintained private Canadian ownership of banking and trust companies, newspapers, and radio and television stations. These measures have, however, been overshadowed by continentalist market forces because the public enterprise tradition has been hedged in by the exigencies of the liberal ideology.

Liberalism, in Canada as elsewhere, has been pulled in two directions. On the one hand its cult of individual freedom, at first limited to a minority of persons, has been gradually expanded to a democratic liberalism in which all persons, theoretically, count equally. But at the same time liberalism has included in its definition of freedom the defence of private property. This has not meant simply property in the sense of personal belongings, but property in the sense of capital, that is, property that can be used as a source of income. Given that property, in this latter sense, is inevitably divided unevenly in the society, there has been a contradiction between the interests of majority control and public enterprise and, on the other side, the interests of those who derive their economic and social position from the private control of capital.

Thus the willingness to use political intervention against market economic forces had to be measured against the possible consequences to the survival of private property and to the stability of the entire social structure. This is the subject of chapter 5.

## Notes

**1.** Walter Gordon (*Storm Signals,* p. 52) states that King entered into informal negotiations on economic integration with the United States. Granatstein's account suggests that King was wary, despite support for the idea from civil servants, including Keenleyside.

**2.** Curiously, Cuff and Granatstein (p. 88) conclude that the economic significance of Hyde Park was "not great, except insofar as it foretold the integration of the North American economies."

**3.** This point and the discussion that follows is developed from an important article by J. Fodor and A. O'Connell, "La Argentina y la economia atlantica en la primera mitad del siglo xx." The article is an analysis of some of the mechanisms of centre-periphery changes as they applied to the case of Argentina, which have some similarities to Canada's.

**4.** The creation of underdevelopment as the result of primary exports has been emphasized by André Gunder Frank. Frank's argument, which has been formulated as a generalization for Latin America, can be briefly summarized as follows: first, Latin America has had a market economy from the beginning of colonialism; second, it has been capitalist from the beginning of its colonial period; and, third, it is the dependent nature of its insertion into the capitalist world market that is the cause of its underdevelopment.

But Frank does not recognize the complexities of the integrative mechanism for each centre country, nor the variety of social structures that can emerge in countries as they are integrated into a capitalist network of trade.

**5.** The fact that the merchants and bankers were based in Montreal and then Toronto has become the basis for a view of Canadian development which can be called "metropolitanism." See Maurice Careless, "Metropolitanism and Nationalism." This approach can obviously be fruitful so long as the national, and international, context is not neglected.

**6.** The U.S. government also found a connection between tariffs and foreign investment, as was seen by the Toronto *Globe* in 1894 when American coal duties were lowered: "It will be noticed how cleverly the Yankees transact their affairs. They want our coal and pass a law to admit it to the United States free of duty. But it will be observed that before passing this law, they had already annexed our most valuable coal mines. ... The removal of their duty on coal is a roundabout way of annexing a portion of our territory." (Quoted by Naylor, vol. 2, p. 176.)

# FIVE
# Canadian Social Structure and the Evolution of Liberalism

The term "liberalism" is rich in meaning, owing its complexity to diverse historical and political usage. For a long time liberalism was associated with a revolutionary movement and was thus regarded with abhorrence in those circles which believed in the divine origins of the status quo. For example, when Sir Wilfrid Laurier addressed his supporters at Quebec in 1877 he had to direct his remarks to people who still worried about "the last king being strangled with the guts of the last priest." Such had been the wish of Jean Meslier (1664–1729), a Frenchman who had evidently been coerced into the priesthood and whose subsequent denunciation of religion was later published by Voltaire. Laurier sought the origins of liberalism in general, and the Liberal Party in particular, in a human propensity for reform. In order to reassure his audience, Laurier appealed to the writings of the English historian Macaulay and his account of the English revolution. England was seen as obviously being on the side of order by virtue of its role as imperial mistress and was frequently advanced as an example of a country where reforms occurred without the bloodshed common in continental Europe. (Laurier's Quebec speech, "Le Liberalisme politique," is reprinted in Sir Wilfrid Laurier, *Discours à l'étranger et au Canada.*)

Macaulay had dated the emergence of political parties in England from the divisions of the Long Parliament of 1641. On the one side were those "anxious to preserve," on the other those "eager to reform." On the one side was "the confederacy zealous for authority and antiquity," on the other "the confederacy zealous for liberty and progress." Thus Tories, the "conservative party," and Whigs, later to be recognized as liberals, had their origins in "diversities of temper." (See T.B. Macaulay, *History of England,* chap 1.) For Laurier, liberals were those men of goodwill who were eager for responsible government, for constitutional government, and for the reform of abuses. Their presence was if anything an antidote to revolution because more revolutions were caused by the obstinacy of conservatives than by the excessive zeal of liberals.

Laurier's view of politics has had a considerable success in Canada. Mackenzie King advanced a similar argument when he referred to politics as a constant struggle of two contending principles, "the principle of the future and the principle of the past" (quoted in F.H. Underhill, "The Development of National Political Parties in Canada," p. 21).

Not all politicians and historians have held this idealistic view of liberalism and conservatism. Donald Creighton, in explaining the political origins of the Conservative Party, suggested that it emerged from the Tory conception of British North America as a "competitive and expansionist entity in the new continent. ... They foresaw an imperialist struggle for the riches of the continent ... [and] their fundamental political principle was unification and centralization of control" ("Conservatism and National Unity," in R. Flenley, ed., *Essays in Canadian History*, pp. 156–57). Some historians have suggested that political principles emerged from the much more mundane interests of politicians. Frank Underhill (*op. cit.*) has argued that Canadian political parties have an essentially "North American" quality in that they are founded on "factions," or private, material interests.[1]

It is not hard to accumulate evidence for this argument. Alexander Galt, prominent nineteenth-century politician and Canadian manager of the British America Land Company, freely admitted that he considered "the interests of the Company and of the country to be identical." The predecessor of Sir John A. Macdonald as leader of the Conservatives, Sir Allan McNab, is notorious for his cheerful assertion that "railways are my politics." (Both are quoted in Underhill.)

While recognizing the weight of the reminder about private interest, it would be wrong to dismiss the claims of King, Laurier, and

Macauley. This does not mean that it would be worthwhile to seek further in the direction of individual temperament to explain beliefs. Rather, it is necessary to look at the structure of the beliefs themselves and the way in which they are related to social structures. In discussing the English Tories and Whigs, Macaulay admitted that the division was one of degree: "There were certain limits on the right and on the left which were rarely overstepped." Those who fought for the Crown "were averse to despotism." The majority of the "champions of popular rights" were "averse to anarchy." Laurier, in his turn, spoke of Liberals as "friends of liberty" but also of "order." He regretted the "youthful" excesses of the group to which he himself had belonged and who had wanted to "change everything." The question that arises is: what defines "despotism" on the one side and "anarchy" on the other? What is "liberty" and with what kind of "order" is it compatible? In the course of its history, liberalism has had to give answers to these questions. The answers have not emerged in abstraction, from the minds of isolated philosophers. They have evolved in the course of social changes which have forced contending parties to define their positions.

Political positions have been conditioned by social organization and thus by the conflicting interests of social classes. In speaking of social classes in this context, it is necessary to take into account the specific forms in which class organizations have appeared and the historical circumstances in which class conflicts have arisen. Class relations are never exactly the same in each country. This important point is made by Edward Thompson, who holds that class is defined by men as they make their own history:

> By class I understand an historical phenomenon. ... the notion of class entails the notion of historical relationship ... [which] must always be embodied in real people and in a real context. Moreover we cannot have two distinct classes, each with an independent being, and *then* bring them *into* relationship with each other. ... The class experience is largely determined by the productive relations into which men are born – or enter involuntarily. Class-consciousness is the way in which these experiences are handled in cultural terms: embodied in traditions, value systems, ideas and institutional forms. If the experience appears as determined, class-consciousness does not. We can see a *logic* in

> the responses of similar occupational groups undergoing similar experiences, but we cannot predicate any *law.* Consciousness of class arises in the same way in different times and places, but never in *just* the same way. (E.P. Thompson, *The Making of the English Working Class,* pp. 9–10)

One of the major factors contributing to the differences in the experience of class relations is of course the national framework within which is passed the lives of the individuals who constitute classes. Clearly the national history of capitalism in any one country constitutes a significant portion of the experiences which contribute to the formation of the cultural values of the various classes in that country. In addition the national framework must be considered in the context of an international hierarchy of capitalist nations, that is, in the world of imperialism. Imperialist relations alter the experiences of classes within both the dominant and the dominated nations, though in different ways.

### *The Emergence of Liberal Society in Canada*

The establishment of liberal capitalist society is not normal or inevitable. Its creation in any given country has to be explained. Furthermore its history is not often the same in peripheral countries as in imperialist countries. In fact its development in peripheral countries is sufficiently unusual to require special attention. In Canada its growth resulted from government policies, particularly with regard to landholding and immigration, and also from the nature of Canadian primary exports and the structure of the industries that grew up around them.

The emergence of liberal society in Europe was the result of a long struggle between two social systems – capitalism and seigneurialism. (The latter term is better than the more commonly used "feudalism," since feudalism designates a particular political system within seigneurialism.) It is impossible to summarize the history of this struggle which was carried on for many centuries and with varying intensity at different times in different countries. It is important, however, to note three points:

1. The triumph of liberal society was achieved after long years of class conflict between bourgeoisie and nobility, and in each country the new liberal society was marked by the particular national form

of this class conflict. This is particularly true of the "superstructural" aspects of each society.

2. The method of transforming agrarian society was at the centre of the conflict.

3. The form of liberal society established has in each case been conditioned by the history of the working class in that country.

With regard to the first two of these points, conditions in Canada were considerably different from those in Europe. First, there was no entrenched seigneurial society of lords and peasants. It is true that in New France a form of seigneurial society had been established, though this was not a simple reproduction of rural European society and it had little of the tenacity of the European variety.

The seigneurial system was adopted in Canada to promote colonization. About 74 per cent of the land went to the laity and the rest to religious orders. In Canada a fief did not confer nobility, though it did bring with it both honorary and real rights. The real rights included typical seigneurial obligations such as *cens, rentes, banalités,* and *corvée,* but the seigneur himself had to work on *corvées* for the *intendant.* The seigneur reserved oaks, mines, and minerals. Unlike the case in Europe, "common land" was granted by the seigneur rather than designated by custom. The emphasis in Canada was on contract and state supervision and in many respects the seigneur was not much more than a rental agent. (See Marcel Trudel, *The Seigneurial Regime.*)

The seigneurial system could not, however, be integrated into the English system of "free and common soccage," and thus British immigrants did not enter into seigneurial land. In Lower Canada they thus settled in the townships, where land was usually colonized by the New England system of grants of large tracts of land to a "leader and associates." The agriculture of the seigneuries was a type of general farming in the early nineteenth century still similar to that of the early eighteenth century, apart from the introduction of potatoes. Wheat was the main cash crop. The *habitants* had moved into commercial society, though their tillage techniques remained largely the old two-year rotation instead of the more modern "convertible" system.[2]

As colonization took place, the relatively scattered native peoples were relegated to small areas of land and their civilizations virtually destroyed. In fact, it was the extent to which the indigenous populations were destroyed in the areas penetrated by European imperialism that largely distinguishes the present-day social structures of these areas. (See, for example, C. Furtado, *Economic Development of Latin America,* parts I and II.) Economic historians have in fact recognized this point, though they have not dealt with it honestly, by referring to some colonial areas as "areas of recent settlement" or "new societies."[3]

There were of course conflicts over land policy in Canada after the Indians had been evicted, but these were conflicts within the framework of an emerging capitalist society and not the result of opposition by pre-capitalist groups. In Lower Canada, the survival of seigneurial property combined with the dominance of the new colonial merchants and government led to the unstable political situation of the 1830's. Even though the struggle was led by pre-industrial social classes, as were many of the democratic struggles in Europe between the 1790's and the 1840's, it was essentially a struggle for a democratic control of the capitalist society that was emerging rather than a struggle against capitalist society.

In a limited, political sense, Upper Canada was a by-product of the American Revolution. The 1791 constitution, if slightly modified in the light of events in the American colonies, represented a continuation of the old colonial system. It was desired in Britain to encourage institutions that would "uphold a distinction of ranks and lessen the undue weight of the democratic influence" as Governor Simcoe put it. British administration in Canada reflected not only the experience of the American Revolution but also the reaction against democracy which the profound shocks of the French Revolution had produced. The government supported clergy reserves and attempted to identify any opposition with the spread of treasonous values from the United States. (See Aileen Dunham, *Political Unrest in Upper Canada, 1815–1836.*)

After the election of 1828, however, the speech from the throne was rejected by a vote of thirty-seven to one. Less than half the Assembly had been born in the United States and discontent was by no means limited to the American element. The fact was that by the 1820's, as William Lyon Mackenzie recognized, the British government, under the influence of Huskisson and "Prosperity" Robinson, was more progressive than the British government in Canada. Mackenzie's brand of liberalism was not alien to Britain, as his connections with Hume and Roebuck suggested, even if Mackenzie sometimes went too far in his appeals to democracy. The constant policy of the radicals in Canada was in fact to blame the local oligarchy and not the British government itself. The problem was not the British connection but, as Mackenzie put it, "the monopoly of power in the hand of a certain class, irrespective of the wishes of the people. ..." (Note: Quoted by Dunham, p. 134.)[4]

The liberalism of the early nineteenth century did not easily accede to democratic claims, as the defeat of Mackenzie shows. To a large extent this was a result of the link between liberalism and the economic theory of market behaviour. The government was able to persuade the majority, or at least the majority of those who were influential, that economic expansion would be threatened by excessively democratic claims. Liberal theory was able to brush aside demands for democracy on the grounds that democracy might threaten property. Economic development, the liberals contended, was contingent upon the maintenance of property. In practice this meant the maintenance of unequal property and the unequal social relations that followed. In response to the question of what sort of government was necessary to the well-being of society, liberalism concentrated its arguments on the theme of economic development. (See C.B. Macpherson, *Democratic Theory.* On changing notions of property see Essay VI. The link between political liberalism and the economic theory of market behaviour is an historical, and not necessarily inevitable, link.)

Yet the achievement of economic development did not reduce the demand for democracy. Correspondingly, the demand for democracy brought into question the claims that economic development benefited everyone equally. A major role in this interaction was played by the political and economic organizations representing the working class.

The process by which this working class developed was not exactly the same as in Europe, because of the colonial nature of Canadian society and its particular form of economic development. In Canada the industrial class structure did not grow on the ruins of an artisan and peasant economy. Industrialization grew to a great extent from the possibilities opened up by the export sector combined with large-scale immigration of people to form an industrial working class. (Of course the working class has also been swelled, particularly in the twentieth century, by the decline of small-scale artisan production and small-scale farming.)

The outstanding fact, however, about Canada, as a colonial area, was the emergence of a working class defined by capitalist production to such an extent that it encompassed the vast majority of the population of the country. Thus, while the key factor in Canada's development has been the extraction of a series of staple products by a series of imperial powers, Canada has never been *merely* a resource colony. Canada was not like other colonies in which capitalism promoted plantation production, using slavery or indentured labour, or perpetuated various forms of non-capitalist production based on peasant labour. Canada has become a fully articulated capitalist society, that is, a society with capitalist property relations, and a society in which the overwhelming proportion of the population is engaged in capitalist production. It is perhaps for this reason that Canada, despite its colonial aspects, has developed into a rich country, but that is also the reason why liberalism has been subject to severe constraints in its adaptation to new social conditions.

*The History of Liberalism*

Liberalism had come into existence in England in the context of demands for a form of government that would defend a new form of property. The new form of property was not associated with status or rank, as land had been, but rather was property associated with labour.

In his *Leviathan* (1651), Hobbes demonstrated the need for a single sovereign power and he argued that this sovereign power was necessary in order to protect the lives and property of men. In fact, without a common power to enforce laws there could be no civilization, because there would be "no place for Industry; because the fruit thereof is uncertain: and consequently no culture of the Earth, no Navigation, nor use of the commodities that may be imported by Sea; no commodious Building; no Instruments of moving and removing such things as require much force; no Knowledge of the face of the Earth; no account of Time; no Arts; no Letters; no Society; and which is worst of all, continuall feare, and danger of violent death; And the life of man, solitary, poore, nasty, brutish and short." (chap. 13, p. 186)

Consider the first sentence. Hobbes says that there would be no place for "industry," that is labour or work, if the "fruit thereof," that is property, was uncertain. Thus without security of property there would be no civilization. An essential part of the liberal argument has always been the claim that property is both the result of labour and the cause of labour.[5]

This argument was taken up by John Locke. In fact, Locke argued quite explicitly that government has no other end but the preservation of property. Locke insisted that government must be concerned with the well-being of society as defined in the here and now:

> We are not born in heaven but in this world, where our being is to be preserved with meat, drink and clothing, and other necessaries that are not born with us, but must be got and kept with forecast, care and labour, and therefore we cannot be all devotion, all praises and hallelujahs, and perpetually in the vision of things above. (Quoted by S. Wolin, *Politics and Vision,* p. 298.)

Both Hobbes and Locke worked out their theories of government in terms of capitalist market societies. But both of them were mercantilists, that is both of them assumed that the regulation of the market was necessary, and in fact desirable, to avoid the disruptive effects of market pressures. The government had a clear responsibility to direct the economic process. This theory, however, eventually gave way to a laissez-faire interpretation of the role of government.

Adam Smith produced a theory of society which assumed, like Locke's, that civil government was instituted for the security of property. That is, government "is in reality instituted for the defense of the rich against the poor, or of those who have some property against those who have none at all" (*Wealth of Nations,* p. 674). But Smith argued that an unregulated, "laissez-faire," economy would provide the best protection against vested interests and result in the greatest well-being of the greatest number. Smith was not, however, as naive as many defenders of the unregulated market, for he recognized very clearly that the market itself was the object of manipulation by class interests. He suggested, for example, that the interests of landlords and wage-earners would coincide, despite the obvious inequalities, since increases in the real wealth of society would increase both wages and rents. But, he suggests, the interest of the third order does not have the same connection with the general interest of society:

> The interest of the dealers, in any particular branch of trade or manufactures, is always in some respects different from, and even opposite to, that of the public. To widen the market and to narrow the competition is always the interest of the dealers. ... They are an order of men whose interest is never exactly the same as that of the public, who have generally an interest to deceive and even oppress the public, and who accordingly, have, upon many occasions, both deceived and oppressed it. (*Wealth of Nations,* Book I, pp. 249–250)

The *Wealth of Nations* is essentially a product of the era before the Industrial Revolution. Capitalism in Britain was only just moving into its industrial phase at the time that Smith was writing, but within forty years the economic structure of Britain had changed appreciably. The Industrial Revolution in Britain occurred at the same time as the political revolution in France. Together the Industrial Revolution and the French Revolution resulted in the sharpening of a conflict over the undemocratic nature of liberal society.

Following the English revolution, Locke had become the authority to which liberals could turn for support. As Leslie Stephen recognized, "that authority vanished when the French Revolution brought deeper questions for solution, and new methods became necessary in politics as in all other speculation" (Leslie Stephen, *History of English Thought in the Eighteenth Century,* vol. 2, p. 114).

There were two strands of opposition to the earlier liberalism. The first was a demand for a democratic form of liberalism which came from the ranks of the pre-industrial craftsmen and small producers whose livelihood was threatened by the growth of large-scale capitalism. These people were the basis for the Jacobin movement during the French Revolution and the contemporary republican movements in Britain. They called for a popular form of government, elected from an active and informed political citizenry. Their movement was ultimately doomed, though its echoes have persisted until our own time, because their support of private property was such as to prevent the effective regulation of the economy, and eventually their economic position was undermined by the growth of industrial capitalism.[6]

These liberal-democratic movements merged with a second form of opposition to liberalism which was produced by the social conditions which resulted from industrial capitalism. The early liberals – Hobbes, Locke, and Adam Smith – had associated property with labour, with work. By the 1820's some people were beginning to ask *whose work* was responsible for the creation of property and whether those who owned property were in fact those who worked hardest. These kinds of questions were posed by the trade unions and workingmen's associations and by the new political movements such as the Chartists, who together formed part of the early socialist movement. It is important to see that these movements were a result of the development of industrial capitalism which had literally created a new working class. (See G. Lichtheim, *The Origins of Socialism*, and E.P. Thompson, *The Making of the English Working Class.*) As a reaction to these new political movements there were many who were willing to abandon the more democratic aspects of liberalism, such as civil rights, in the defence of property. This was demonstrated most clearly in France, both after 1793 and again following the revolution of 1848. Liberalism, which in its earlier years had been relatively frank about the class nature of property and did not make any claims to democracy, underwent a transformation. (See C. B. Macpherson, *Democratic Theory,* Essay XI, on the decline of liberal theory.)

With the emergence of the artisan, working-class, and socialist opposition, liberalism split into various strands. Some liberals who insisted on the primacy of the market organization of society departed from their liberalism in some respects by grafting on some elements of the "Darwinian" interpretation of society, which made possible an argument that society was "just" while being manifestly unequal. Some liberals, who insisted on the need to maintain market principles, nevertheless argued that in fact society was becoming more equal and even more socialist. The point, this group said, was to allow this evolution to occur slowly, thus avoiding unnecessary disruption. There were also some liberals who tended to become pragmatic about the role of the market in ordering economic activity and social organization and who allowed some grounds for regulation of the market or redress of inequalities.[7]

Some of these strands can be seen in the mid-nineteenth century within the work of John Stuart Mill, one of the major figures in the evolution of liberal thought. Despite his failure to overcome the constraints of classical economic theory, Mill was the first liberal to take seriously the claims of democracy; and he was sufficiently deeply disturbed by the moral evils of the market society to take seriously the socialist attack on it.[8]

In 1869/70, when Mill wrote his essay on socialism, he was aware that the institution of private property had to be defended. If nothing else the recent extension of the franchise in Britain had admitted to the vote a great number who were

> not engaged ... by any peculiar interest of their own, to the support of property as it is, least of all to the support of inequalities of property. So far as their power reaches ... the laws of property have to depend for support upon considerations of a public nature, upon the estimate made of their conduciveness to the general welfare. ..." (*Collected Works.,* vol. 5, p. 706)

Mill was also aware of the appalling consequences of industrialization for the working class, and the poverty in which that class remained.

> No longer enslaved or made dependent by force of law, the great majority of them are so by force of poverty; they are still chained to a place, to an occupation and to a conformity with the will of an employer, and debarred by the accident of birth both from enjoyments and moral advantages which others inherit without exertion independently of desert. (*Ibid.,* p. 710)

The working class was entitled to claim, Mill concluded, that all social institutions be re-examined. If the institutions were not all susceptible of change, conditions of life were. In another essay ("Claims of Labour" – the title of a book he reviewed) Mill acknowledged that many were enquiring "how the great mass of the people are fed, clothed and taught – and whether the improvement in their condition corresponds at all with the improvement of the condition of the middle and upper classes. And many are of the opinion [that it does not]." Mill went on to say the concern with this question was "salutary and promising" but "it would be idle to suppose that it has not its peculiar dangers. ... Society cannot with safety, in one of its gravest concerns, pass at once from selfish supineness to restless activity. It has a long and difficult apprenticeship yet to serve."

Mill assumed that the laws of capitalist production were rooted in nature and biology. He was unable to see the extent to which they were in fact social laws, susceptible of change. He thus failed to see that it was capitalism that entailed the market relations between individuals which limited their personal development and placed limits on the prospects for social progress. Such prejudices were reinforced as liberal economic theory, following Mill, concentrated on the concept of marginal utility and was held to have proved that the market maximized utilities with regard to consumption and rewards for effort.

Professor C.B. Macpherson has suggested that the weakness of the now popular liberal democratic theory, which begins with Mill and also T.H. Green, lies in its retention of the concept of man as an infinite consumer and infinite appropriator. The insistence on individual property rights means in effect a denial to most men of equitable access to the means of life and the means of labour (Macpherson, *Democratic Theory,* Essay IX).

Those who followed the more conservative side of Mill's arguments emphasized the essential condition of sanctity of private property. This is the case with Lord Acton, for example, whose ideas have been influential in Canadian liberalism. (A recent example is found in the thought of Pierre Elliott Trudeau. See A. Rotstein, *The Precarious Homestead,* chap. 8, pp. 107–11 esp.) There was, however, a strand of the new democratic liberalism which showed a much greater willingness to contemplate control of market mechanisms and to use the power of government to remove many of the abuses created by industrial capitalism. This led to demands for what was later called a "welfare state" in opposition to the often excessive, money-seeking individualism that characterized the late nineteenth century.

### *Evolving Liberalism and Canadian Politics*

The Canadian government in the last century did not show any enthusiasm for reforming its liberalism in the direction of democracy. In 1870, Sir John A. Macdonald made it clear that he still regarded the defence of property to be the major concern: "The great question to be asked in deciding whether or not a man shall exercise the franchise, is whether or not he has a sufficient stake in the country to be entrusted with a share in its government." (Quoted in C. Berger, *The Sense of Power,* p. 203. Macdonald's political views are discussed by Peter Waite, "The Political Ideas of John A. Macdonald," in Marcel Hamelin, ed., *The Political Ideas of the Prime Ministers of Canada,* pp. 51–67.) Macdonald was suspicious of democracy and sceptical about the possibilities of reform. He believed in the association of power and property to the extent that he wanted the Senate to represent property as a check to a more democratic House of Commons.

Yet, despite Macdonald's reluctance, it was clear that Canadian society was changing in such a way that the achievement of any form of democracy would require a modification of the automatic association of power and property. At Confederation less than 15 per cent of the labour force was in manufacturing and handicrafts, but wage labour was becoming the usual experience of a rapidly growing number of Canadians. And those men and women, and even children in those days, who depended on wage labour for their livelihood did not own property, and were not likely to, in the sense in which Macdonald understood the term.

Even in the largely rural society of the earlier nineteenth century wage labour was not uncommon.[9] Not all Canadians established themselves as "pioneer" farmers owning their own land or as merchants or artisans owning their own businesses. Even in the fur trade the majority of *coureurs de bois* had worked as wage earners for the great companies which from early days dominated the trade. In lumbering some men relied on their wages for year-round support, while some had two jobs, working on their farms, or their father's farms, in the summer and working in the *chantier* in the winter. For much of the nineteenth century, in the Maritime colonies and in the Canadas, farming was a major activity, but not all those who worked on farms owned their own land.

When Catharine Parr Traill and Susanna Moodie established themselves in the "backwoods" of Canada, they came as the wives of English officers entitled to land grants and as the sisters of a wealthy farmer who had preceded them to Canada. But Catharine Parr Traill comments on the fact that "poorer" immigrants, even those who could acquire land of their own, were obliged to "hire out" and "suffer much privation before they reap the benefit of their independence." There were some who never reaped the benefits. Susanna Moodie speaks of her "bare-legged, ragged Irish servants," and though she often complains of the "independence" and "high wages" of the small number of "suitable" servants, the important point was the existence of such a class of servants. They were even more numerous in the towns and cities.

By the 1840's the problems of the industrial revolution were beginning to reach Canada. The creation of a modern working class was the result of nineteenth century economic development. As H.C. Pentland puts it:

> The capitalistic labour market ... is the one so well supplied with labour that employers feel free to hire workers as desired, on a short term basis without assuming any responsibility for their overhead costs. There is not much sign of such a market in Canada before 1830. In the next two decades there is evidence of transition towards it. ... The essential structure of a capitalistic market existed in the 1850's, and the market had attained some sophistication by the 1870's. ( "The Development of a Capitalistic Labour Market in Canada," p. 455. See also his "The Lachine Strike of 1843.")

The new conditions of employment posed serious problems. The introduction of machinery and the regimentation of workers in large numbers under the control of employers fundamentally changed the nature of work. Workers protested in Canada in the same way as they had elsewhere. The protests tended to begin with outright refusal of the new conditions, as for example in the 1840's when Montreal shoemakers smashed sewing machines, and progress to a more organized effort to exercise some control over the inevitable changes. The 1843 Lachine canal workers' strike was a herald of the change, though the trade union movement did not become firmly established in Canada until the 1860's.

It was obvious that social conditions were changing to such an extent that new attitudes to society were necessary. Not only did working conditions require new forms of organization, but the combination of urbanization and a laissez-faire liberal attitude to social questions was producing dismal and unsanitary living conditions for large numbers of working people. Overcrowding and lack of sewerage became characteristic of the growing cities. More and more men and women were working in factories, but the modification of liberal attitudes was much slower than the social reorganization because laissez-faire suited the immediate interests of those who were powerful.

The change to a more regulated society has been interpreted in various ways. Karl Polanyi, for example, in his study *The Great Transformation*, argued that a market organization of society was incompatible with social survival, particularly insofar as labour could not be readily made into a commodity. Polanyi saw the opposition to laissez-faire liberalism as a necessary protective reaction by "society." But such social changes were by no means automatic and to suggest they were is to neglect the crucial role played by courageous individuals and groups who, in the face of often savage repression, fought for changes that would humanize society. The maintenance of human values was not achieved without heavy costs, borne frequently by people unknown to historians.

George Brown and the Toronto *Globe* were typical of the employers' response to demands for change. First they argued that Canada was already sufficiently democratic: "We have no such class as those styled capitalists in other countries. The whole people are the capitalists of Canada. ... Not only are the people at large the real capitalists of Canada. ... The people have entire political power in their own hands. ..." (M. Cross, ed., p. 169) Yet when Toronto printers challenged the *Globe*, George Brown had the strike leaders arrested on charges of conspiracy. In fact it was only in 1872 that a Trade Union Act was introduced to legislate that the mere fact of combining to increase wages or reduce hours of work was not a conspiracy and did not violate the common law. Even then trade union organizers could still be subject to harsh treatment by anti-union judges and found guilty of seditious conspiracy.

The *Globe* continued to attack the "injudicious zeal and not over enlightened benevolence" of those who wanted to introduce welfare measures, and opposed the regulation of hours of work of those over fourteen years of age. But laissez-faire did not work equally in both directions. Labour relations were regulated by laws such as the Masters and Apprentices Act which made employees liable to imprisonment for absenting themselves without permission, or for disobeying the orders of employers.

In company towns, and in the mining areas especially, the treatment of workers was even harsher than in the larger centres. The government intervened on the side of employers with armed force. Laurier told the House of Commons that labour was advancing its position in Canada: "At last labour has been advanced to the dignity of a class in itself, and quite as important in the economy of society as any other class" (quoted in R.C. Brown and R. Cook, *Canada 1896-1921,* p. 119). It was the same prime minister who ordered troops into action against miners. At the time of the 1909 Glace Bay strike, the President of the Bank of Montreal wrote to Laurier: "Permit me to congratulate you on your prompt action in sending troops to Cape Breton. It is undoubtedly saving riot, bloodshed and much destruction of property, and as we have large interests in that section of the country, we have reason to be thankful." (Quoted *ibid.*, p. 117) Businessmen who were far from averse to combining with each other to guarantee "a living profit" were strong in their belief that trade unions were an attack on liberty. (See Michael Bliss, *A Living Profit: Studies in the Social History of Canadian Business, 1883-1911,* esp. chap. 4.)

Yet by the early twentieth century, some politicians and a few businessmen were beginning to modify their liberalism in the face of new conditions. There were several strands to the "reform" movement. The new techniques of business organization and financing in the late nineteenth century had led to a concern that "the American speculative element" was bringing business into disrepute. The creation of spectacular fortunes and the ostentatious flaunting of wealth, combined with the tales of stock-watering and financial manipulation, made it too easy to see that wealth did not come from savings and hard work. The more sober elements of the propertied class began to worry that "the common people" would be provoked to respond.[10]

Some churches, notably the Methodist church, played a significant role in changing social attitudes and bringing about a recognition of the limitations of competitive individualism. The "social gospel" movement began in a concern with immigration and slum conditions and the sense that growing numbers of industrial workers were staying away from the churches but the movement led many of its participants into a radical questioning of the nature of their society. While retaining the evangelical impetus, the reformers examined such decidedly secular subjects as labour relations, the control of industry and wealth, and the possibility of a democratic society. (See Richard Allen, *The Social Passion; Religion and Social Reform in Canada, 1914–1928.*)

The municipal reform movement also contributed to the changing climate of opinion. It was apparent that some public services were necessary and that market forces would not produce satisfactory urban conditions. Battles over urban services actually led further in some cases, as with Adam Beck and the "public power" movement which created the demand for Ontario Hydro. Beck countered the complaints of laissez-faire liberals with an appeal to democracy:

> I do not understand that any revelation has ever been made from Heaven to the effect that a democratic government commits an unpardonable sin when it assists in the establishment of a great and necessary public work for the well-being of the people of whose interests it is the trustee.

(Note: Quoted in Brown and Cook, p. 106. On Adam Beck and Ontario Hydro see H.V. Nelles, *The Politics of Development*, chaps. 6 and 7. One aspect of the response of the private power companies was to call on such English liberals as Goldwin Smith and A.V. Dicey, who contributed to a pamphlet called *The Credit of Canada.* Dicey had attacked "collectivism" in his *Law and Public Opinion in England.*)

Programs for reform reached the level of national politics in Borden's 1907 "Halifax platform" (R.C. Brown, "The Political Ideas of Robert Borden," in M. Hamelin [ed.], pp. 87–106). Borden argued for a greater economic role for the federal government, not only in regulating and controlling but also in owning and initiating activity. The public domain should include, in addition to natural resources, "national franchises" and public utilities, such as telegraphs and telephones, run for the benefit of the whole population.

Laurier, and also many on Borden's side of the House, remained committed to a more individualist view of society.[11]

Yet there were those who, without being in the "public enterprise" tradition of Beck and Borden, recognized that the demand for change could not be denied. It was a question of what sort of changes should be made. In this light, O.D. Skelton, then Professor of Political Science at Queen's University, took the trouble to write a lengthy critique of socialism. (*Socialism: A Critical Analysis.* The book was the winner of the Hart, Schaffner, and Marx prize for an essay on "The Case against Socialism.")

Skelton did not believe that the socialists were a major force in Canada, since "widespread poverty is unknown" and "the gates of opportunity are open wide" (p. 309). He devoted only one page of his book to socialism in Canada which, he claimed, was associated with "the motley foreign quarter" in Winnipeg, though he did note its existence in Montreal, Toronto, and the mining areas of Cape Breton and British Columbia. Skelton's view was that private property would survive because self-interest, "the most powerful and abiding force in human nature," could thus be "harnessed to the social good" (*ibid.*, p. 42). But liberals would have to recognize that the defence of private property required that the social good be ensured through government regulation. Private property, he suggested, could be moralized by developing a sense of wealth as a trusteeship, socialized by the extension of joint-stock ownership, and democratized by trade-union sharing in determining the conditions of employment (*ibid.*, p. 310).[12]

Thus the need for change was seen in diverse circles in the early twentieth century. Yet ultimately it was war that forced the changes. The war led to the limited beginnings of government social services, although most social service work was still privately organized (Brown and Cook, chap. 12). But perhaps the most significant fact was, as Stephen Leacock said, that the war "taught new things about possible financial burdens" (quoted *ibid.*, pp. 302–3). It was demonstrated that the government was capable of mobilizing immense forces and reorganizing society. The government raised money through the new Income Tax and Business Profits Tax; it established national factories for war production and virtually created an aircraft industry; and it regulated food and fuel supplies. There were many who were determined that the sacrifices of the war would not be in vain.

The government was forced to recognize the growing strength of the trade union movement during the war. In 1918 a "War Labour Policy" was enunciated, which, while preventing strikes and lockouts, did express a belief in the eight-hour day, fair wages, and equal pay for equal work by women.[13]

The trade union movement appeared to be in a critical phase in 1918, being tugged by some towards socialism or syndicalism, being urged towards business unionism by others. Demands for social reconstruction, for industrial democracy and the co-operative commonwealth were bringing trade unionists into contact with farmers organizations and social reformers of a variety of persuasions. In the labour churches such men as William Ivens and J.S. Woodsworth preached a Christianity that was progressive, scientific, practical, and above all, social. The Methodist General Conference, meeting in Hamilton in 1918, called for labour democracy, extensive nationalization, and comprehensive social security. The present economic system, it was argued, "stands revealed as one of the roots of war." (Note: See Allen, *chap. 4.* On Woodsworth, see K. McNaught, *A Prophet in Politics.*) By 1920 Salem Bland, in his *New Christianity*, was arguing that protestantism could be identified with "bourgeois Christianity" and that a new epoch was arriving in which labour values would be to the fore. The RCMP kept the more radical Methodists under surveillance and brought pressure on the church leadership to control them (Allen, chap. 4).

The Canadian Reconstruction Association, a big business lobby, worried about the dangers of an alliance between labour and farmers for economic changes. Sir John Willison, president of the CRA, wrote to an associate: "If we lost Labour the industrial system of this country cannot survive." (See Tom Traves, "The Story that Couldn't be Told.") The CRA's policy, in addition to courting individual trade unionists, was to urge employers to recognize unions and negotiate and to explain that tariffs and the National Policy would create jobs and prosperity.

The Winnipeg General Strike added an element of urgency to the debate. (See D.C. Masters, *The Winnipeg General Strike.* Norman Penner has edited a collection of documents in *Winnipeg, 1919.*) The strike was suppressed with the use of considerable force and prison sentences, but the discontent remained. In October 1919 the United Farmers of Ontario formed a provincial government, and in January 1920 the National Progressive Party was established in Winnipeg.

The man who attempted to pick up all the pieces was William Lyon Mackenzie King. King dominated Canadian politics in the 1920's and 1930's, and his views can be seen as a bridge between the liberalism of the late nineteenth century and that of the mid-twentieth century. He portrayed himself as a politician who understood labour relations and the new problems associated with industrialization. In his youth he wrote articles on the sweating system and slum conditions in Toronto and he had gained experience of settlement work at Jane Addams' Hull House in Chicago. He acquired first-hand knowledge of settling strikes as Canada's first deputy minister of labour, and then minister of labour, and during the war years worked for John D. Rockefeller who was looking for new solutions to the labour problems in his industrial empire. In *Industry and Humanity,* published in 1918, King tried to chart a path for liberalism in the aftermath of the catastrophe, and, incidentally as it were, to put himself forward as the helmsman. (The best study of this is H.S. Ferns and B. Ostry, *The Age of Mackenzie King.*)

King emphasized the theme of society as a partnership. There are four partners: the capitalists who make available their wealth; managers who organize capital and labour; labour which produces under direction; the community which sustains the whole apparatus of production (*Industry and Humanity*, chap. 5). What was new in King's liberalism was his emphasis on management as the key to the future and his raising of the "public interest" to the overriding criterion for social judgment. What was not so new was his interpretation of the "public interest." Ultimately, despite King's claim that he heralded a new era in social relations, his analysis offered no solutions to the social conflict which grew out of private ownership and wage labour. (See Ferns and Ostry, chap. 9, and D.J. Bercuson, Introduction to 1973 reprint of *Industry and Humanity.*) He appeared to be willing to consider "industrial democracy," but he actually avoided even the question of union rights. He did not expect management to concede any of its powers. In fact King's liberalism was sufficiently old-fashioned that he had little faith in merely social institutions. His idealism was directed towards a "spiritual interpretation of life," and his optimism outweighed by a Calvinistic sense that only some individuals, and certainly not whole societies, might be elected to grace. (Ferns and Ostry, chap. 9 and Allen, p. 199). Social improvement was ultimately limited by imperfections in human nature and thus King could picture himself as a reformer without expecting too much change, and without challenging too many interests.

It has often been claimed that King's political genius was to occupy the ideological centre while appearing to conciliate both left and right. He excluded socialists from the Liberal Party while appearing to make Toryism the enemy.[14]

Conciliation was not, however, the main characteristic of Canadian liberalism in either the 1920's or the 1930's. Depression and conflict were more typical. In western Canada farmers experimented with a variety of political alternatives: the United Farmers of Alberta, Social Credit, the Progressive Party, the Co-operative Commonwealth Federation. Not all the supporters of these movements had by any means rejected liberalism, but it was apparent that the prevailing liberal economic policies of Canadian governments were inadequate to the times.[15]

Throughout the country people were still embroiled in conflicts for trade union recognition. If it was true that legislation emphasized compulsory intervention in labor disputes, compulsory intervention favoured employers more than unions. (See Stuart Jamieson, *Times of Trouble: Labour Unrest and Industrial Conflict in Canada, 1900–1966,* p. 53.)

Entire communities still found themselves confronted with force – employed in the name of "peace, order and good government." As Jamieson concludes (p. 269), the "frequency with which governments invoked force and violence ... particularly in breaking up unemployed demonstrations, and in helping employers break strikes, tended to generate an image of governments as oppressor. It perhaps encouraged a widespread contempt for the law as an entity designed to protect property rather than human rights."

Liberalism had gone through a period of turmoil, but, if the golden age of the bourgeoisie was over, the age of capital was just suffering from one of its periodic bouts of depression.

## Notes

**1.** The view to which Underhill subscribes was developed in the United States by James Madison. The tradition survived in the work of historians such as Beard. The more cynical proponents of the school turned to "muck-raking," as in the case of Gustavus Myers who introduced this side into Canada in his *History of Canadian Wealth.*

**2.** See G.F. McGuigan, "Administration of Land Policy and the Growth of Corporate Economic Organization in Lower Canada, 1791–1809," and R.L. Jones, "French-Canadian Agriculture in the St. Lawrence Valley, 1815–1850." In the 1840's there was a turn to oats, peas, and barley after the devastation wrought by the wheat midge; and then, in the 1850's more livestock was introduced. For farming in Ontario at this time see R.L. Jones, *History of Agriculture in Ontario, 1663-1880.* For a description of the revolutionary changes that had occurred in British agriculture by this time, see J.D. Chambers and G.E. Mingay, *The Agricultural Revolution.*

The seigneurs of Lower Canada did not lose their *domaines* when seigneurial tenure was ended in 1854. At that time the *censitaires* either paid a lump sum equivalent to the market value of the land or continued to pay rent. Most of them remained in debt. In the late 1930's these farmers became debtors to the municipalities rather than to the descendants of the seigneurs.

**3.** On early land treaties, see P. Cumming and N.H. Mickenberg, *Native Rights in Canada.* For an evocation of the later situation in western Canada, see the powerful novel by Rudy Wiebe, *The Temptation of Big Bear.* For the north, see René Fumoleau, *As Long as this Land Shall Last.*

**4.** As Dunham points out, the themes of nationalism and democracy linked Upper Canada to both Europe and the United States. The Canadian Radicals generally had a program similar to the British Benthamites, who believed that colonies were unnecessary and too expensive. In the colonies the seventeenth-century parliamentary practice was still in effect, thus creating conflict between executive and legislature. Even in Britain, however, the responsibility of the government to Parliament was still not clear. It was not emphasized by Blackstone, and Montesquieu's interpretation had stressed the separation of powers, rather than the concept of responsibility. In fact, in Lower Canada the lawyers in the assembly who in the first decade of the century had promoted their opposition views in *Le Canadien* had learned to frame their arguments in terms of Blackstone and Locke, rather than the revolutionary "rights of man" arguments, to avoid the accusation of treason. (See Lawrence Smith, "*Le Canadien* and the British Constitution, 1806–10").

**5.** On the interpretation of "labour" in Hobbes, see C.B. Macpherson, *The Political Theory of Possessive Individualism*, and also his introduction to the Pelican Classics edition of *Leviathan*. It is clear that already for Hobbes and Locke the term "labour" implied "initiative" in setting others to work. An opposing view was held by Winstanley. (See C. Hill, *The World Turned Upside Down.*)

**6.** As mentioned above, it was the opposition of small-scale producers to the survival of seigneurial property, to the privileges of the Crown and the Church, and to the dominance of the new colonial merchants, which led to the unstable political situation in Canada in the 1830's. With appropriate modifications, a similar movement emerged among farmers in this century, when small-scale agriculture was under pressure from economic conditions and vulnerable to banks, railroads, and farm equipment companies.

**7.** Some of the ground for this latter position had been prepared by the Utilitarian version of liberalism which had been present from the start, even in some of the apparently "natural law" versions. See E. Halevy, *The Growth of Philosophic Radicalism.*

**8.** Mill recognized that socialism was "a designation under which schemes of very diverse character are comprehended and confounded but which implies at least a remodelling generally approaching to the abolition of the institution of private property." ("Chapters on Socialism," *Collected Works* vol. 5, pp. 704–53.) "Thoughtful" and "philosophic" socialists followed Owen and Fourier. The "revolutionary" socialists of the continent proposed that the working class should manage all productive resources through a central authority.

**9.** There is no comprehensive history of nineteenth century work or the formation of the Canadian working class. A mixed collection of documents is reprinted in M.S. Cross, ed., *The Workingman in the Nineteenth Century.* Selections from the 1889 Royal Commission on the Relations of Labour and Capital, edited by G. Kealey, have been reprinted. See also S.M. Trofimenkoff and A. Prentice, eds., *The Neglected Majority,* and S. Langdon, "The Emergence of the Canadian Working Class Movement, 1845–75," *Journal of Canadian Studies,* vol. 8, 1973.

**10.** See M. Bliss, *A Living Profit*, chap. 1. Stephen Leacock mocked the new wealth and the pretensions of the Montreal establishment in *Arcadian Adventures of the Idle Rich.* The concern with "declining" business and social standards was evinced in other countries. See, for an English example, Trollope's novel, *The Way We Live Now.* Looking back at the period, Thomas Mann, in *Buddenbrooks*, examined the reaction of the old merchant elite in northern Germany to the new rapacious financiers.

**11.** Arthur Meighen, for example, showed that support for tariffs, Ontario Hydro, the CNR, and the supervision of corporate affairs did not necessarily go with deep-rooted feelings about democracy. Meighen was responsible for the repressive legislation concerning "aliens" during the First World War, and, by the 1930's at any rate, was of the opinion that it was "exceedingly doubtful if democracy can survive universal suffrage ... for any great length of time." (See R. Graham, "Some Political Ideas of Arthur Meighen," in M. Hamelin, ed., pp. 107–20.)

**12.** On the role of trade unions in income distribution, Skelton showed a pragmatic liberalism uncommon at that time. He regarded income distribution "as a matter of bargaining power, of relative indispensableness, of ability to make good a claim to sharing by the threat of withdrawal" (pp. 207–8).

**13.** Women had been playing an increasingly important political role. The women's suffrage movement won the vote in Manitoba in 1916. By 1922 women voted in federal elections and in all provinces except Quebec. Many women had become active through the temperance movement and the social gospel. See Nellie McClung, *In Times Like These.* Stephen Leacock suggested that prohibition had unfortunate consequences. The drinkless worker would angrily demand luxuries, harbour envy, and attack social inequalities. "See to it that he doesn't turn into a Bolshevik" (quoted by Allen, pp. 268–69).

**14.** See for example, H.B. Neatby, "The Political Ideas of William Lyon Mackenzie King," in M. Hamelin, ed. pp. 121–37. In this context Toryism meant colonial-minded and protectionist big business. J.W. Dafoe suggested that the Liberal Party should move more clearly into the centre, dropping its "non-democratic wing," which was more closely allied with the Conservative Party. "Reality" in Canadian politics, he suggested, could only be achieved by a re-alignment – "the left-wing of the Liberals joining up against a combination of the right-wing of the Liberals and the Conservatives" (See W.L. Morton, *The Progressive Party in Canada,* p. 260).

**15.** See, for example, C.B. Macpherson, *Democracy in Alberta: Social Credit and the Party System.* Macpherson shows how Social Credit in Alberta was "related to the needs of a society that was politically and economically a subordinate part of a mature capitalist economy, and whose people at the same time had preponderantly the outlook and assumptions of small-propertied independent commodity producers."

# SIX
# Contemporary Society

By the 1930's it became apparent to some liberals that government regulation had to be extended to cover economic instability. The theoretical rationale for this view was developed by John Maynard Keynes. There was a similarity between Keynes and Mill when it came to the precise nature of regulation. In an essay entitled "The Economic Possibilities for our Grandchildren," Keynes, sixty years after Mill, made the same kinds of criticism of the capitalist economy and projected his hopes for a better future. Yet Keynes dismissed the alternatives with remarkable cynicism. "Avarice and usury and precaution must be our gods for a little longer still. For only they can lead us out of the tunnel of economic necessity into daylight." *(Essays in Persuasion,* p. 372) Because of the changed social conditions, however, Keynes went much further than Mill had in his concessions about the role of government in the present. By this time it was not merely socialists who thought that the future of capitalism was problematic. Keynes pointed to the dangers inherent in a belief that the clock could be set back:

> The gold standard with its dependence on pure chance, its faith in "automatic adjustments," and its general regardlessness of social detail, is an essential emblem and idol of those who sit on the top tier of the machine. I think they are immensely rash in their regardlessness, in their vague optimism and comfortable belief that nothing really serious ever happens. Nine times out of ten, nothing really serious does happen – merely a little distress to

> individuals or to groups. But we run a risk of the tenth time (and are stupid into the bargain), if we continue to apply the principles of an economics which was worked out on the hypothesis of laissez-faire and free competition, to a society which is rapidly abandoning these hypotheses. *(Essays in Persuasion,* p. 262)

Keynes wrote this in protest at Churchill's return of Britain to the gold standard at an unrealistic value for the pound. As he noted the coal miners were the first to suffer the consequences and he worried that "unless we are lucky" they would not be the last. The 1926 General Strike suggested what the further consequences might be.

The old liberalism had to be replaced by "liberal socialism." Keynes used this term to refer to "a system where we can act as an organised community for common purposes and to promote social and economic justice, whilst respecting and protecting the individual – his freedom of choice, his faith, his mind and its expression, his enterprise and his property" (quoted in D.E. Moggridge, *Keynes,* p. 44). The chance for survival lay in the abandonment of laissez-faire policies. Liberal economic theory and policies had to be modified by the recognition that government action was necessary to achieve an acceptable equilibrium position, since the market equilibrium might be undesirable with regard to the level of unemployment.

Keynes thus provided much of the ideological justification for the "new" economic role for capitalist governments. In concluding his analysis of twentieth-century capitalism, Keynes wrote:

> I conceive, therefore, that a somewhat comprehensive socialisation of investment will prove the only means of securing an approximation of full employment; though this need not exclude all manner of compromises and of devices by which public authority will co-operate with private initiative. But beyond this no obvious case is made out for a system of State Socialism which would embrace most of the economic life of the community. It is not the ownership of the instruments of production which it is important for the State to assume. If the State is able to determine the aggregate amount of resources devoted to augmenting the instruments and the basic rate of reward to those who own them, it will have accomplished all that is necessary.

Moreover, the necessary measures of socialisation can be introduced gradually and without a break in the general traditions of society. *(The General Theory of Employment, Interest, and Money,* p. 378)

*The "Mixed Economy"*

The Second World War finally put an end to the years of depression, but during the war years there were many government officials who worried about the return to normalcy. Graham Towers of the Bank of Canada felt that the federal government would have to control corporate and personal income taxes and take responsibility for dealing with unemployment. In 1940 he wrote: "Is it not likely that workers will face unemployment in the post-war period with much greater resentment – to put it mildly – than displayed during the depression years? In the interests of peace, order and good government the Dominion may well have to assume full responsibility." (Quoted in J.L. Granatstein, *Canada's War,* p. 163.) The Liberal government groped cautiously towards the introduction of social measures, spurred on occasionally by fears of the manifest strength of the CCF.

Leonard Marsh of McGill University, who had worked with William Beveridge in England and who was a member of the League for Social Reconstruction, submitted a report to the government in 1943. The *Marsh Report* argued that unemployment must be the main concern of social security, that social security must be underwritten by the community as a whole, and that public works projects must be undertaken if necessary to create full employment. In addition, Marsh recommended government programs of child allowances, health insurance, and pensions. King was of the opinion that these policies were too far-reaching, but public pressure was mounting. In 1943 a public opinion poll showed the CCF to be the most favoured party with 29 per cent of the poll, against 28 per cent each for the Liberals and Tories. In August 1943 the CCF captured 34 seats in the Ontario election, and in June 1944 they won the Saskatchewan election with 47 out of 52 seats. Furthermore the overseas vote of servicemen showed majority support for the CCF. King persuaded his cabinet to produce a Throne Speech in 1944 which was based on Marsh's report.[1]

During the war years the Conservative Party also underwent a reexamination of its beliefs. J.M. Macdonell, the President of the National Trust Company, called for a new national policy with social security, based on full employment at a decent wage as the main goal. The alternative, Macdonell suggested, was frightening: "Would you rather adopt a policy which will retain the largest amount possible of free enterprise or – hand over to the CCF ...? Half a loaf is better than no bread." (Granatstein, p. 251) In order to emphasize that they were remaining in the vanguard of liberalism, the Conservatives restyled themselves Progressive Conservatives in 1942 and endorsed social insurance, full employment, collective bargaining, and medical insurance. [2]

Whether as a result of government policies or as is more likely, as a result of the new international situation, the Canadian economy did not return to depression following the war. The costs of the new round of developments were, however, the loss of a large measure of national sovereignty.

As Canada became a victim of the shifting power structure of the North Atlantic triangle and fell under the dominance of the United States, a common way of denying the reality of the situation appeared: this was to take refuge in the notion that Canada was in any case a natural candidate for Americanization and, far from losing anything, was in fact finally reaching its destiny.

Since Canada was a wealthy country it was possible to rejoice in the fact that we shared the "American way of life." It was possible to celebrate the inherent qualities of such a life:

> Everywhere in the twentieth century man is becoming American, or to put it another way, is moving in some way towards a condition of high industrialization, affluence and leisure, instant communication, an urban man-made environment, and a mingling of cultures and traditions in a mobile, classless, global society. There is no country in the world, except the United States, which has gone further in this direction than Canada. ... (W. Kilbourn, ed., *Canada: A Guide to the Peaceable Kingdom,* p. xiii)

The notion of Americanism was frequently associated with that of classlessness. As in the United States, it was argued that this country was tolerant, broadly egalitarian, by and large affluent, and above all classless. The purveyors of this view argued that Canada was essentially classless because everyone was more or less "middle class" by virtue of a high-level, standardized consumption of automobiles, television sets, household appliances, clothing, vacations, and sporting facilities. The "more or less" qualification allowed for the fact that some were a little less "middle class" because they consumed a little less of these things, while some were a little more "middle class" because they consumed a little more of them.

In conjunction with this view it was argued that the growth of government had offset the unequal distribution of power which results from ownership of property to such an extent that power was equally shared among citizens. It was also argued that the growth of government power had been such that it was no longer correct to consider Canada to be a capitalist country. The capitalist economy, it was said, had been replaced by a "modern", "western", "industrial", "mixed", or even "socialist" economy.[3]

The ideologists who have developed the concept of industrial society have argued that we are in a "post-liberal" society. Thus, while there may be "class" divisions, they are not related to the ownership of capital. According to George Lichtheim, one of the more sophisticated of these ideologists; "Class as a socio-economic concept belongs to the bourgeois age, and it is questionable whether it can be made to work under circumstances where property in the means of production is no longer the characteristic line of division between the major groups in society" *(Marxism,* p. 382). He goes on to say that "the emergence of new forms of dependence and control, both under corporate management and state controlled planning, has 'sublated' the historical antagonism of capital and labour, and established a new perspective from which to view the conflict of classes" *(ibid.,* p. 392).[4]

One thing that is clear, however, is that the extension of citizenship and increased regulation by the government does not result in genuine equality. The fact that the factory manager and the assembly line worker are both citizens does not make them equal throughout the working day which is itself a major part of their lives and which determines much else of their existence.

Democracy has been instituted as a form of government but not as a condition of society. The distinction follows from the inequality of property, since the holding of property confers power over those who do not own property. And further, the system of government, which is ostensibly based on a theory of equality of opportunity, in fact sustains inequality through its support of unequal property relations. (See C.B. Macpherson, *The Real World of Democracy* and R. Miliband, *The State in Capitalist Society.* Property is here, as in previous chapters, used not to mean personal belongings but property that can be used as capital.) As Ralph Miliband's study of the nature of modern government puts it:

> The economic and political life of capitalist societies is *primarily* determined by the relationship, born of the capitalist mode of production, between ... two classes – the class which on the one hand owns and controls, and the working class on the other. Here are still the social forces whose confrontation most powerfully shapes the social climate and the political system of advanced capitalism. In fact, the political process in these societies is mainly *about* the confrontation of those forces, and is intended to sanction the terms of the relationship between them. (*The State in Capitalist Society.* p. 16)

As a result of social pressures the role of governments and the living conditions of the majority have changed markedly. But the changes occurred, as Keynes had envisaged, without a break in "the traditions of society." These changes have not yet altered the basic social framework of capitalism in Canada. In fact many of the changes in government economic activity have been clearly designed to support profit-making by private corporations. "Private enterprise" has found some aspects of the "welfare state" necessary to its own survival. The Quebec Federation of Labour (FTQ) complained of this in their manifesto of the early 1970's: "... under the liberal state, public financing injected into the economy is given outright to private capital, or supports it so as to raise profit ratios. This strengthens the private sector at the expense of the public sector." ("The State is Our Exploiter," translated in D. Drache ed., *Quebec – Only the Beginning,* p. 210)

Canada has not become an egalitarian, classless society. There remain substantial inequalities and furthermore these inequalities are linked to class structure. A series of studies of incomes have shown that not only is income distribution unequal but that many Canadians actually live in what can only be described as poverty.[5] The report of the Special Senate Committee on Poverty showed that, even after transfer payments such as welfare benefits have been received, almost 40 per cent of non-farm family income goes to only 20 per cent of the total number of families, while an equal number of families at the other end of the scale receive only about 7 per cent of the total income. And this pattern of unequal distribution has been almost constant for the last two decades. (See the Report of the Special Senate Committee on Poverty, *Poverty in Canada;* also Ian Adams and others, *The Real Poverty Report.)* More recent studies have shown that the situation has not improved since the Senate Committee study. Transfer payments have not reduced inequality, but have at most held that inequality constant. (See W. Irwin Gillespie, "On the Redistribution of Income in Canada.")

In its 1968 review (p. 104), the Economic Council of Canada disposed of many of the myths concerning poverty:

> Many Canadians may assume that the problem of poverty is close to identical with the problem of low average incomes in the Atlantic Provinces and Eastern Quebec (especially their rural areas) and among the Indian and Eskimo populations. But this is an inaccurate impression. The *incidence* of poverty – the chance of a given person being poor – is certainly much higher in the areas and among the groups just mentioned. But in terms of absolute numbers, between a third and a half of total poverty in Canada is to be found among the white population of cities and towns west of Three Rivers.

The Council's review also provided some figures to combat the notion that poverty is simply the consequence of misfortune, lack of effort, or personal inadequacy (p. 113). In 68 per cent of low-income non-farm families there were adults who were in the labour force for at least part of the year. In 76 per cent of the group there were *one or more* income earners in the family, and 66 per cent of the families obtained most of their income from wage, salary, and self-employment earnings. In 77 per cent of the families there were adults under 65 years of age. And in 87 per cent of the families in the group there were adult men.

The conclusion that emerges is that many Canadians are poor *despite* the fact that they work. The Economic Council also warns us against the assumption that bad wages are found only in a small number of occupations. It is true that the incidence of low incomes is high for farm workers, loggers, and fishermen, but families including farm workers, loggers, and fishermen account for only about 10 per cent of low-income families (Table 6–4, p. 115).

There is a further study that should be just mentioned here since many people assume that the tax structure redistributes income away from higher incomes towards lower incomes. In fact, as the 1966 Report of the Royal Commission on Taxation (the Carter Commission) showed, Canadians suffer from a regressive tax structure. That is, taxes take away a higher proportion of income from the low-income receivers than from the high-income receivers. Individuals are not taxed according to their ability to pay. As Gillespie's 1976 study showed, tax incidence is regressive up to an income level of about $5,000 and then again beyond $15,000, while being proportional in between.

Most of the studies of poverty and inequality did not come to terms with the reasons for the situation. The existence of economic inequality in a country as rich as Canada is linked to fundamental features of the social structure. The class divisions which exist in Canadian society correspond to unequal divisions of economic power and opportunity. In *The Vertical Mosaic,* a study of Canadian social structure which has become widely accepted, the sociologist John Porter demonstrated that it was wrong to believe that Canada was either "classless" or was a "middle-class" society. Canadian society, he concluded, was marked by fundamental inequalities, and Canada "has a long way to go to become in any sense a thoroughgoing democracy" *(The Vertical Mosaic,* p. 557). Porter documented the existence of a series of elites in various sectors of Canadian society, which owed their positions to inherited wealth and power. Furthermore, the evidence suggests that these elite people function as a dominant class. (Porter did not reach this conclusion, but there are reasons for disagreeing with him. See J.A. Hutcheson, "Class and Income Distribution in Canada," pp. 58–64.)

There are many people who accept this analysis but assume that the educational system can produce changes in the social structure. There is evidence, however, that the expansion of education in the 1960's did not have this effect. It could not, for example, offset the social results of the organization of the economic structure. Corporate concentration has increased in the years since Porter's study. According to Statistics Canada, in 1971 as few as 291 firms controlled 58 per cent of capital assets, produced 30 per cent of the goods and services, and collected 39 per cent of the total profits in the corporate sector of the economy. Concentration is particularly marked in mining, primary metals, and manufacturing. (See Eric Kierans, foreword to T. Naylor, *The History of Canadian Business, 1867–1914.*)[6]

The results of the further concentration of economic power have been documented by Wallace Clement (*The Canadian Corporate Elite; An Analysis of Economic Power*). According to the evidence of Clement's study the significant directorships were even more exclusively an upper-class preserve than had been the case at the time of Porter's enquiry. Of the 673 Canadian-born members of the economic elite, 28.5 per cent had fathers, or in a few cases uncles, who had been members of the economic elite. A further 2.4 per cent had fathers who had been in the political elite. A further 5 per cent had married into elite families. A further 15 per cent had attended private schools, and another 10 per cent had fathers who, while not having quite reached the elite, had been substantial businessmen. Thus about 60 per cent of the elite could be considered to be from the upper level of society. Of the rest, about 8 per cent of the total had fathers in the professions. Of the remaining 30 per cent, the majority had attended university – at a time when only about 8 per cent of their age group had done so. In fact only about 2 per cent of the elite had entered the economic elite through building up their own businesses. The inequality of power increased in the 1960's.

In Canada, it is possible to divide the economic elite into internal and external components. The internal elite itself consists of two sections. The first is the "indigenous" elite who are the directors of Canadian-owned corporations. The second section of the internal elite is made up by the directors of branch plants operating in Canada. Some of them are Canadians, some foreigners resident in Canada. The external elite consists of the directors of the multinational corporations outside Canada which control the branch plants. Thirty per cent of the elite positions *within* Canada are held either by U.S.-born individuals or by employees of U.S.-owned corporations whose appointments are controlled from the United States.

The truncation of the Canadian economy by multinational corporations has meant that many of the top decision-making positions in the Canadian economy are held by non-Canadians and by those who work in foreign-controlled corporations. The appointment of personnel to positions in the branch plants is made by a foreign elite, a large portion of which consists of members of the U.S. elite. The directors of branch plants do not make the most significant decisions in their corporations, though their decisions are of profound significance for Canada.[7] They in fact play the role of managers rather than that of owners. Thus the real decision-making power in the Canadian economy is divided amongst the indigenous elite and the external elite who control the multinational corporations operating in Canada. The indigenous elite dominates the financial institutions and transportation, while U.S. corporations dominate the resource sector and manufacturing.

The existence of an "indigenous" elite which controls the service sector of the Canadian economy does not negate the fact that Canada has become a dependent country. In fact, the indigenous elite may well have fostered a form of development that brought about dependency. The power of the "indigenous" elite may reside precisely in the fact that it is willing to commit itself to a continentalist economic policy.

*Economic Problems*

Continentalism is seen by many to be a successful economic policy, even if some people may recognize that there are political costs and occasional strains in our relationship with the United States. But in fact there is a very large body of literature that suggests that continentalism has very serious economic drawbacks. Continentalism has perpetuated a reliance on resource exploitation and a corresponding retardation of secondary manufacturing. Continentalism means economic dependency.

An important contribution to theories of economic dependency and underdevelopment was made in the early 1960's, as the staple approach to Canadian history was being formalized into a staple theory, or model, of economic development. In 1963 Professor Mel Watkins published an article called "A Staple Theory of Economic Growth" which developed the theory as one of capital formation. At the same time G.W. Bertram emphasized the point that the staple model could be seen as a theory of regional growth within the framework of an international economy. (See G.W. Bertram, "Economic Growth in Canadian Industry, 1870–1914: The Staple Model and the Take-Off Hypothesis.")

Watkins pointed out that a fundamental assumption of the staple theory was that staple exports acted as a "leading sector" of the economy. One could then ask what "spread effects" are caused by the leading sector. Spread effects can be analyzed more precisely by identifying a series of "linkages." The purpose of the concept of linkage is to show how developments in the export, leading, sector changed other sectors of the economy. Watkins identified three types of linkage. "Backward linkage" is a measure of the inducement to invest in the domestic production of inputs, including capital goods, for the expanding exports sector. "Forward linkage" is a measure of the inducement to invest in the industries using the output of the export sector as an input. The third type of linkage, "final demand linkage," is a measure of the inducement to invest in domestic industries producing consumer goods for factors in the export sector.

Using these concepts, it is possible to make an assessment of how any particular export industry has, or might in the future, generate other forms of economic activity within the country. If the export sector creates strong linkage effects of all three types then general economic growth will occur at a higher rate than if some or all of the linkage effects are weak. Watkins drew attention to two types of problems that might arise in an export-led economy. First, the linkages might be sufficiently weak to produce what is known as an "enclave" economy. That is, the export sector, while itself developing rapidly and possibly with a high level of technology, might have virtually no effect on the rest of the economy. The export sector could remain, in effect, a part of a foreign economy. The second problem is that an economy could become caught in a "staple trap." Economic factors might accumulate excessively in the export sector and thus be unavailable for other types of activity. This could leave the economy highly vulnerable to a sudden shift in the fortunes of the export sector and also limit the scope of actual economic progress.

This latter point was also considered by G.W. Bertram. Bertram pointed out that for a staple economy the international context is of major importance. In particular the staple economy is dependent on events elsewhere. The demand for the export staple is clearly an "exogenous" factor. That is, the demand originates outside the country and fluctuations in demand cannot be controlled within it. Secondly, while the export staple is likely to be a natural resource, resources can only be exploited in accordance with technological possibilities, and technological change is also likely to be an exogenous factor in a staple economy.

It is clear then that the economic development of a staple economy cannot be considered independently of the economies which absorb the staple product and which may provide the technology and economic organization for the exploitation of the staple. Finally we should recognize that economic activities also have social and political ramifications. For example, Watkins, in accordance with the then current theories of economic development, added a concern for the quality of entrepreneurship that might exist in a staple economy, Canada's in particular. But even this is too narrow a focus. Entrepreneurship, like other economic qualities, is not a random factor. It is an aspect of social structure that is strongly affected by economic organization as well as being one of the determinants of economic organization.

Professor Kari Levitt has emphasized the connection between entrepreneurship and forms of economic organization. In her view, the multinational corporations have created a new mercantilism:

> In the new mercantilism the corporation based in the metropolis exercises the entrepreneurial function and collects a "venture profit" from its investment. ... The competitive strength of the modern multinational corporation ... lies in the superiority of its marketing and business organization which enables it to create monopoly-type venture profit by expertise in product innovation and want-creation. (*Silent Surrender: The Multinational Corporation in Canada*, p. 24)

As Levitt suggests, the problems arising from the impact of multinational corporations in fact go far beyond the questions of entrepreneurship. The problems can be classified as economic, political, and cultural.[8]

The behaviour of multinational corporations has profound consequences for the structure of the Canadian economy. In the years from 1967 to 1969, the foreign sector of the Canadian economy controlled about 35 per cent of total corporate savings. Thus the foreign sector exercised an enormous influence on the pattern of investment in Canada. The production patterns of U.S. subsidiaries have in fact resulted in inefficiency in Canada. The Canadian market is only 10 per cent of the American market, and there has been an uneconomic proliferation of firms and products as competing American corporations have spread into Canada.

Thus the Canadian economy is made up of foreign- and domestic-owned firms which have a different level of productivity from industries in the United States and elsewhere. Despite the fact that U.S. corporations in Canada are not more efficient than Canadian corporations, U.S.-owned manufacturing firms continue to dominate the Canadian economy through the benefits of marketing, advertising, managerial, and technical economies which result from their relationship to their parent corporations. For the same reasons, foreign ownership limits innovation as branch plant managers lack the incentive, and the freedom, to develop autonomous industry. Both domestic technology and domestic management skills are suppressed. Finally, as a result of the relationship with the parent corporation, subsidiaries create a continental trade pattern in which 70 per cent of Canada's import and export trade is with the United States.

A multinational corporation is not concerned merely with the growth of a particular subsidiary, but rather with the growth and profitability of the corporation as a whole. Decision-making is shifted outside of Canada into the head offices of the corporations. This not only has economic consequences but also political ramifications. It conditions the relationship between the Canadian and the U.S. governments. It frequently introduces American political concerns into Canada, as a result of the "extraterritorial" extension of U.S. laws on trade, for example. Canada's balance of payments situation may be weakened by export restrictions placed on subsidiaries or by the insistence of multinational corporations on a high degree of interaffiliate trade, which may require purchasing in the United States. This alienation of decision-making seriously reduces the ability of the Canadian government to control economic growth, standards of living, and employment levels.

In addition, foreign investment locks Canada into American society in a cultural sense. Foreign direct investment is a "package deal," bringing not just capital, but the management outlook, the products, and the marketing behaviour of American corporations. It is often argued that Canadian consumers "prefer" this kind of society, but in fact most of the decisions are made within the corporations and are not the result of "consumer sovereignty." (See, for example, J.K. Galbraith, *The New Industrial State*.)

Some people would recognize the existence of these problems but would still argue that foreign direct investment is necessary to create economic growth in Canada. The need for this form of investment, however, is not so obvious as might be thought. It is difficult to be precise about this because first there is the problem of measuring the relationship between growth and investment. To what extent is the rate of economic growth related simply to investment and to what extent is it related to "technical progress" and "productivity changes?" There is no clear answer, and neither is it certain that multinational corporations have a better record than domestic corporations with regard to technical progress. Secondly, to what extent is the level of investment increased by the presence of multinational corporations? Here the answers are clearer and they are not necessarily in favour of the multinationals.

A high proportion of investment by U.S. corporations in Canada is the result of the internal savings of the Canadian subsidiary. Perhaps, on average, as much as 60 per cent of the new investment is the result of earnings in Canada and is thus actually "Canadian" saving. Another source of U.S. corporate investments in Canada is borrowing in the Canadian financial market, which again is the result of Canadian saving. According to the *Gray Report* (Tables 7, 8), between 1946 and 1967, about 78 per cent of the financing of foreign-controlled firms was obtained from internal savings and capital acquired in Canada. Thus, from 1946 to 1967, only about 22 per cent of financing was obtained from foreign sources, and this proportion dropped to 19 per cent in the 1960's.

In the case of a foreign take-over of an existing Canadian corporation there is no immediate increase in real investment; neither is there necessarily any eventual new investment resulting from the release of funds to be used elsewhere in the Canadian economy. Payment for a take-over is usually in the form of a share swap in which no new capital need enter the country. As the *Gray Report* points out, even in the event of a cash payment the transfer may be offset by the action of the Bank of Canada, which may have to buy foreign exchange to stabilize the value of the Canadian dollar. (For a further discussion of the "transfer problem" see Lukin Robinson, "Who Pays for Foreign Investment?")

There are other aspects of Canada's balance of payments situation which are related to foreign investment. Canadian savings may need to be diverted from new investment to pay for a current account deficit resulting from past foreign investment. The *Gray Report* estimates that U.S. direct investments have an aggregate deficit impact on the Canadian balance of payments after ten years. In the 1960's there was actually a net outflow of capital from Canada (Levitt, p. 94). Yet at the same time foreign ownership increased markedly as the result of Canadian savings controlled by foreign corporations.

Finally, foreign direct investment may have had a detrimental effect on the development of the capital market in Canada. (See the *Watkins Report*, pp. 267–94.) Foreign investment may have suppressed domestic capital formation. A case in point is the history of the Ford Motor Company of Canada Ltd. The company was founded in 1904 by a Canadian with an initial capitalization of $125,000, of which 51 per cent was given to the Ford Motor Company of Detroit in return for all Ford rights and processes in Canada and other parts of the British Empire. Between 1905 and 1927 the company paid cash dividends of close to $15 million and increased its capital almost entirely by way of stock dividends. (See H. Marshall, F.A. Southard and K.W. Taylor, *Canadian-American Industry*.)

Thus it is not possible to reply to critics of multinational corporations simply with the answer that Canada "needs" this form of foreign investment. In fact the *Gray Report* suggested that a full employment level of investment could have been financed within Canada in the early 1970's. The Canadian government has, however, continued to reject its own reports concerning the problems of foreign direct investment. It has instead pursued economic policies that promoted foreign capital formation in Canada and thus tied Canada's economic growth to resource exports.[9]

In Canada, as Harold Innis noted long ago, banking and finance, transportation and government activity have all been directed to resource exports and the industrial needs of the imperial economy.

*Continentalism and Nationalism*

It is clear that the division between nationalists and continentalists is fundamental with regard to policies for the future. The gulf was exemplified in the positions embodied in two publications that appeared in 1975. One was a study by the Economic Council of Canada, entitled *Looking Outward.* The other was a book by Walter Gordon with the title *Storm Signals.*

According to the ECC, Canada can be characterized as an advanced industrial nation but it is a relatively small economic unit, "lacking the domestic scope for enhanced efficiency through large scale specialization in the manufacturing sector" (p. 2). In addition there is a problem of slow productivity growth.[10] Thus Canada's ability to compete is limited. A basic cause of poor performance in manufacturing, the ECC contends, is the commercial policy adopted by Canada and other countries. The study suggests that "though not so extreme as in earlier years, our present commercial policy retains a strong element of protectionism ... " (p. 24).

Several European countries now have a higher per capita national income than Canada. The ECC accepts the view of several studies that the causes of this are related to the limitations on productivity imposed by small market size. Average Canadian plant size is significantly below that of Britain, West Germany, the United States, France, and Sweden. The problem of market size has been worsened by the tariff barriers which artificially divide markets. Furthermore, tariffs have contributed to foreign direct investment by encouraging foreign manufacturers to produce within the tariff boundary. Thus our commercial policy has reduced productivity without providing economic independence. The tariff is also found to be at the root of the problem of regional inequality. Approximately 80 per cent of manufacturing employment is in Ontario and Quebec. The ECC draws the conclusion that the Canadian tariff in fact imposes a tax on other regions to the benefit of Ontario and Quebec. The study does admit, however, that in the automotive industry, which is of significant size in Ontario, nominal duties are only 1.6 per cent and thus not a major factor in its location.

Looking at the prospects for international trade in the coming years, the ECC sees the growing importance of trading blocs, which implies that countries excluded will have little chance of success.

The Council also points to the probability that primary commodities will be in short supply. Canada is well situated to supply primary commodities but "the resource industries alone are unlikely to provide sufficient high-grade employment for an increasingly educated labour force" (p. 60). Thus primary exports must be bolstered by further processing in Canada, which is possible if productivity can be improved. Again the answer to the problem is trade liberalization.

The ECC expects that the result of trade liberalization will not be harsh as far as manufacturing is concerned, though "demand policies" and direct government assistance would be needed to offset unemployment. (See chap. 13. On p. 82 they suggest that the results of gradual tariff reduction have not been very satisfactory.)[11] The ultimate result is likely to be "regional specialization" in the "North American economy" with some areas of Canada doing well as long as Canadian wage gains relative to the United States are offset by productivity increases. Canadian manufacturing productivity, they suppose, would move up to U.S. levels, thus raising the standard of living permanently to a new level. Trade liberalization for Canada in fact means free trade with the United States and a further continentalization of the Canadian economy. (See pp. 99-101 and chap. 9.) The ECC hopes that Canada's own multinational corporations will grow in the invigorating climate of "regional specialization." The example they themselves give of existing "free-trade specialization" is the Canada-U.S. Automotive Agreement, or Auto-Pact.

The Auto-Pact has indeed created a continental North American automotive industry. A 1973 study of multinational corporations by the U.S. Senate reported that in fact the U.S. entered the Auto-Pact precisely in order to prevent the evolution of a Canadian auto industry. (See W. Gordon, *Storm Signals*, pp. 30–33.) Canada accounts for more than 12 per cent of the North American market; yet only 6 per cent of auto-parts are made in Canada, less than 4 per cent of 1974 investment was in Canada, and employment in the Canadian auto industry has fallen by 23,000 since the Auto-Pact was introduced, according to a study by the U.S. International Trade Commission.

The Economic Council recognizes some of the well-documented problems of American ownership, such as inefficiency, lack of innovation, and the limitation of trade with countries other than the

United States. The study even suggests that foreign ownership has been a bad effect of commercial policy. Even if it is true, however, that foreign ownership in the past has been encouraged by the tariff, the removal of the tariff is unlikely to reduce it. In fact the ECC states that in the short run U.S. ownership of Canada would increase in the event of free-trade (see p. 111). In a continental economy "free trade specialization" as a solution to foreign ownership is simply removing the boundary that makes the U.S. corporations foreign.

An alternative view of new economic policies for Canada is provided by Walter Gordon, former minister of finance, in his book *Storm Signals*.[12]

Gordon takes the position that under a free-trade arrangement between Canada and the United States, most new manufacturing plants would be built not in Canada but in the United States. He also cautions against the assumption that a transfer of population from manufacturing to the service sector would engender prosperity, even if it were a practical proposition to transfer the jobs of one or two million people. In fact the service sector is passive, "depending largely for its expansion on other sectors of the economy" (p. 53). Thus manufacturing is a key to the Canadian future. But U.S. corporations in Canada export raw materials and import manufactured goods that could be produced here. In addition to the economic imbalance that this creates there are political consequences. The Canadian economy, Gordon points out, is becoming increasingly vulnerable to the decisions of the U.S. government, especially as the U.S. government attempts to protect the position of the U.S. in a changing international economy. In other words, multinational corporations not only produce the problem of control by the U.S. corporations, but also that of control by the government of the United States. The result is doubly disturbing for the prospects of democracy in Canada.

We must, Gordon tells us, define a new economic policy. Canada now has a mixed economy and has the advantage of not being "so wedded to a system of 'free-enterprise' as our friends to the south of us" (p. 26). This is important because in defining an economic policy one of our problems will be our relations with the United States as that country runs short of raw materials and is tempted to rely more and more on Canada to meet its needs. In 1972 a Joint Committee of the Senate and House of Commons reported on the constitutional changes that should be made if Canada is to cope with the economic problems posed by foreign control and influence. The Joint Committee suggested that the federal government would need greater power to deal with the multinational corporations and the power of the United States. It seems clear that a comprehensive new national policy would be needed.

## Notes

**1.** Earlier in the war, King recorded the opposition within his own party to unemployment insurance proposals. "Howe has very much the employer's mentality. Ilsley is just blind with prejudice. Ralston has set his whole mentality in the direction of keeping down expenditures. ... He has been closely associated with large corporations and is out of touch with the social trend." (Granatstein, *Canada's War,* p. 253) Later, when Pickersgill was arguing the necessity of family allowances, Howe remained opposed on the grounds that they would "encourage idleness." Howe was, however, in favour of a partnership between government and industry for "reconstruction."

**2.** Though the party remained uncertain and divided on these measures. Charlotte Whitton led the Conservative reaction to the *Marsh Report.* Meighen, who had lost his attempt to re-enter Parliament when in 1942 he was defeated in York South by the CCF candidate, was still complaining in 1943 that "You cannot Beveridge a country into prosperity" (quoted in Graham, p. 114).

**3.** Canadian sociology was influenced in this respect by the assiduously perpetuated myth of the total social uniqueness of the United States. Many Americans have felt the need to deny that the socialist critique of capitalism could ever apply to the United States, nor, probably, by extension, to Canada. Contemporary American sociology has added that it no longer applies to "post-liberal" Europe, and that economic development will soon render it inapplicable in the "third world." The prevalence of American sociology in Canada has not only resulted in the rejection of socialist views but also of non-socialist Canadian approaches to Canadian society.

**4.** "Sublated" is a useful word. It suggests both destruction and preservation, thus enabling Lichtheim to have his cake and eat it too. See also Lichtheim, *The New Europe*, and also the writings of Schumpeter and Galbraith. An alternative revision of the concept of class has been offered by Georges Gurvitch who uses a concept of class "structuration" which allows for the temporary waxing and waning of class organizations under varying historical circumstances. See the discussion in A. Giddens, *The Class Structure of the Advanced Societies.* See also, T. Bottomore, *Classes in Modern Society* and *Marxist Sociology.*

**5.** The problem of establishing an adequate standard for the measurement of poverty is discussed in the 1968 *Annual Review* of the Economic Council of Canada. Before the rapid inflation of the 1970's, a rough dividing line would have been an income of $2,000 per year for an unattached individual and $5,300 per year for a family of five. Even conservative estimates suggest that at least one-quarter of the population is living in poverty.

**6.** Kierans argues that in fact the federal government has "provided the major impetus to corporate concentration in this country." The corporate tax structure favours the largest firms as the result of tax exemptions and privileges. Since 1971 Canadian corporations have been allowed a full deduction for interest paid on money borrowed to buy shares in other corporations. Roughly then, other tax payers have made a 50 per cent subsidy to the cost of take-overs.

**7.** See Clement, pp. 116–21, and also the *Gray Report.* Clement suggests (p.118) that the "powerful elite associated with U.S. direct investment is actually a foreign elite more appropriately described as a parasite." Clement's discussion of the indigenous elite is curious. He recognizes that their position depends on a continentalist economic strategy (pp. 345–55) and he also suggests that the indigenous elite might have stifled the development of Canadian manufacturing and resource industries. Clement however comes to the remarkable conclusion that the Canadian elite is not in a dependency relation with a foreign elite, but is independent (p. 201). The "core" of Canadian capitalism is not weak, he suggests, only the "periphery" has been sold off to U.S. corporations (p. 217). It is certainly an enviable economy that can regard manufacturing and resource industries as a "periphery." Clement's suggestion that the partnership of the Canadian elite with U.S. corporations is an equal partnership, rather than a junior partnership (p. 357) simply ignores the realities of economic development.

Clement acknowledges that elite theory often concentrates too much on social mobility and ignores economic functions and class relationships (pp. 33–40). But he ignores this point in his conclusions. There is an inherent risk in the elite theory approach to power that the functions of the owners of capital will be personalized. As Marx noted, it is "only because his money constantly functions as capital that the economic guise of a capitalist attaches to a man" (*Capital*, vol. 1, chap. 23). The actions of corporate directors are primarily influenced by their function as owners of corporations which operate in an economic context which they cannot modify from day to day. The indigenous elite of the past did not have to commit itself to a continentalist policy but the present structure of the Canadian economy has made a reversal of this policy extremely difficult for the present elite and they are now in a dependent position since they cannot control the pace, or nature of, economic development in manufacturing and resources.

**8.** The subject has been dealt with in two important government-sponsored studies. The first was the "Watkins Report," *Foreign Ownership and the Structure of Canadian Industry*, the Report of the Privy Council Task Force on the Structure of Canadian Industry. The second was the "Gray Report," *Domestic Control of the National Economic Environment: The Problems of Foreign Ownership and Control.* On technological weaknesses resulting from foreign ownership, see P.L. Bourgault, *Innovation and the Structure of Canadian Industry*. Many of the points made in these studies are acknowledged by the Economic Council of Canada in its 1975 study, *Looking Outward,* pp. 34–35.

**9.** The Foreign Investment Review Agency, FIRA, which was set up following the *Gray Report*, has generally had no effect on foreign investment. This point has been made in diverse places. See, for example, the report by the Canadian-American Committee, *A Time of Difficult Transitions: Canada-U.S. Relations in 1976*, and also the article by Ian Urquhart, "The Welcome Wagon," *Macleans,* 1 November 1976. For an analysis of resource exports and policies to offset the situation, see Eric Kierans, *Report on Natural Resources*

*Policy in Manitoba.*

**10.** The statistics show that output in the decade from 1960–70 grew at an annual rate of 5.2 per cent, which compares favourably with other countries (except Japan at about 11 per cent). To a considerable extent, the ECC concludes, this rise was a result of the rapidly growing labour force. The average increase in output per person was only 2.3 per cent. This figure is similar to the United States and the United Kingdom, but lower than several western European countries and Japan, which ranged from 4 per cent to 10 per cent. Canada's output per man-hour remains some 20 per cent below that of the United States. (See *Looking Outward*, Table 6–4, p. 75. The real net output per man-hour in manufacturing in Canada in 1972 was 78.2 per cent of that in the United States. This reflects a gain in Canada over the United States from 72.8 per cent in 1963. This change has partly been caused by the improvement of Canada's terms of trade and the appreciation of the dollar.)

**11.** The ECC does deal with the question of whether trade liberalization might create unemployment in Canada. Manufacturing employment now accounts for about 20 per cent of employment, though only 15 per cent of total employment is in manufacturing with more than 5 per cent tariff protection. This figure is surprisingly low in virtue of the burden which tariffs have earlier been made to carry in explaining inefficiency. Assuming that the labour force will grow more slowly in the late 1970's and 1980's, even if the worst happened to Canadian manufacturing it "would apply only to a relatively small number of Canadian workers" (p. 64). Afraid that some people might not regard "only" 15 per cent as quite so insignificant, the Council hastens to add that the service sector, which now has 63 per cent of the labour force, can be expected to grow. In fact, the "modern trend" is towards the "post-industrial" economy where the emphasis is on the production of "intangibles." Canada should have a "comparative advantage" here because of its highly developed educational system. In estimating the tariff-dependent employment at an upper level of 15 per cent the study does not appear to consider indirect employment. A study done in the 1950's estimated that from 1928 to 1953, roughly 3 out of every 10 additional jobs were provided by the protected manufacturing industries. See Clarence L. Barber, "Canadian Tariff Policy," p. 522.

**12.** In the 1950's Gordon headed the Royal Commission on Canada's Economic Prospects. In 1966 he wrote *A Choice for Canada: Independence or Colonial Status* and when he was president of the Privy Council he commissioned the Task Force on Foreign Ownership and the Structure of Canadian Industry. Gordon notes (*Storm Signals*, p. 79) that the Economic Council has "well-known continentalist leanings" and he takes issue with some of their assumptions. In particular, he points to the fact that continentalism is associated with a belief in the "validity of neo-classical economic theory as applied to Canada" (*ibid.*, p. 52).

# SEVEN
# A New National Policy?

In his 1963 Massey Lectures, Professor Frank Underhill discussed the hopes that existed at the time of Confederation for a new nationality. The nationalism of the time, which he identifies with the "liberal-romantic" view of nationalism and the nation state, gave rise to such phenomena as the Canada First Movement.[1] But, practically, the new national sentiment was "canalized" by Macdonald in the National Policy and the building of the CPR. The National Policy followed as a declaration of economic independence. The National Policy succeeded, Underhill suggests, because of the support of business interests, including railway promoters, bankers, manufacturers, land companies, and contractors. It was in fact "a policy carried out under the leadership of, and for the primary benefit of, a group of great capitalist entrepreneurs working in close alliance with the national government. We have since then made no fundamental modifications in this form of society." (F.H. Underhill, *The Image of Confederation,* p. 62)

Professor Underhill believed that the National Policy has had unfortunate consequences. It created regional inequalities and also set an unfortunate example of corruption as a result of the alliance between business and government. But he also believed that the opposition forces that in the past have called for a new national policy, the Progressives and the CCF, failed because of their limited view of the problem. A new national policy, Underhill claimed, cannot be found in "protectionism" but only "in the world community."

What Canada needs is an "Adam Smith or a Cobden" (p. 64). To suggest that these two gods of the liberal pantheon could provide the inspiration for a new Canadian national policy does indeed in one sense mark a break with the old policy. In the old policy the idea of protection, embodied in the tariff, was what virtually became equated with the Canadian nation itself, being seen as both a barrier to continentalism and a declaration of fiscal autonomy from Britain – as Professor Craig Brown points out in "The Nationalism of the National Policy."

Yet in another sense the old National Policy was both founded on liberalism and destroyed by external forces which were unopposed as a consequence of the adherence to liberal policies. The challenge posed by Underhill is to find the basis for a new national policy. His own answer suggests the magnitude of the problem.

*The Nationality of Canada*

A national economic culture and national economic policies presuppose some consensus concerning the values of the nation which supports them. They presuppose a degree of nationalism which creates at least an awareness of the loss suffered in the absence of such a culture and such policies. Social and economic changes have in fact produced new forms of nationalism in Canada. But as a result of the historical circumstances surrounding the creation of the country, two nations have emerged within Canada, one English-speaking, the other French-speaking. At times they have existed as "two solitudes." At moments of truth, such as the aftermath of the Riel rebellion, the conscription crises of both world wars, and the War Measures Act of October 1970, they have returned to the position of the 1830's: "two nations warring in the bosom of a single state." The manner in which Quebec has been integrated within Canada has given rise to a new Quebec nationalism, which is supported by social groups whose position has been formed by the economic changes of the twentieth century, and which is in opposition to the present Confederation.[2]

The challenge implicit in Confederation, to produce eventually one society and a new nationality, lay not only in the problem of regional equality, but perhaps more fundamentally in the need for the mutual recognition of the equality of the two nations which had been united in Canada. The problem was that many English-speaking Canadians hoped that French-speaking Canadians would become a minority and that the federal government would at most protect their minority rights. This concept of Canada had been clearly established in the 1830's, through a combination of the efforts of British policies and the demands of English-speaking settlers.

British policy with regard to Canada in the 1830's was defined by the Colonial Office as resting on three principles. One was to maintain a connection between the two countries as members of the same monarchy. The second was to maintain an outlet for poor emigrants. The third was to maintain the commercial interests that were a result of the colonial character of the Canadas, New Brunswick, and Nova Scotia. (See Peter Burroughs, *The Canadian Crisis and British Colonial Policy, 1828–41,* p. 81.) The need for an outlet for surplus population was emphasized, though of course this policy tended to produce results that were in contradiction with the other principles. As the population of Upper Canada grew, going from approximately 158,000 in 1825 to 791,000 in 1850, so did the expectations that it would achieve a greater degree of political autonomy.

The new nationalisms of French-speaking and English-speaking Canadians were created in the 1820's and 1830's and were shaped by the events that culminated in the rebellions of 1837. The conflict was complicated by being at the same time an internal social struggle, a national conflict, and a crisis in imperial relations, sharpened by the British government fears that Americans would intervene as they had recently in Texas.

The English-speaking Canadian view of the 1837 conflict has been, by and large, similar to that put forward by Professor Creighton. Creighton saw the events as a clash between agriculture and commerce, accentuated in Lower Canada by the obscurantist efforts of French-speaking Canadians to preserve an unprogressive and semi-feudal society, while the merchants were attempting to build a modern, viable, and independent economy. It was a clash between classes and nations: "The French Canadians, a pastoral people dominated by professional groups, were in most essential respects Frenchmen of the *ancien régime;* the British, whether bureaucrats or *commerçants,* were typical products of the age of industrial revolution and of *laissez-faire.*"[3] The social conflict had been brought out by the changing economic conjuncture of the 1830's. The shift from fur and timber to wheat and flour exports was dislocating the Canadian economy. The new products required a commercialization of agriculture, whereas the fur and timber trades had not challenged seigneurial agriculture.

Creighton argued that the new colonial structure had created a new governing class. The Chateau Clique and the Family Compact were not so much a "company of blood relations" as a "fraternal union of merchants, professional men and bureaucrats." The Reformers on the other hand drew support from the countryside. In Upper Canada especially, the Reformers attacked government spending and voiced their opposition to the banks and land companies. There were national differences: "In Lower Canada, which was still devoted to subsistence agriculture and to a debased feudal land-holding system, the peasants' opposition to commercialism was deepened by a touch of archaic misunderstanding and hatred. But in both provinces there was the same struggle against the institutions and programmes of the commercial class and the same dislike of commercial wealth and privilege." (Creighton, in Easterbrook and Watkins, p. 224) This interpretation points to many of the social forces at work in the 1830's. But Creighton's view of the Canadiens, though convenient for English-speaking Canada, is too simplistic. First the feudal system was not so much of a barrier as he suggests. (See chap. 5 above.) And secondly he misinterprets some of the reasons for opposition to "progress." By implicitly assuming that commercialization and the national subordination of French-speaking Canadians was both inevitable and desirable, Creighton caricatures the commonly found and understandable reactions of a rural population to the appearance of a capitalist agriculture dominated by other people. (There is a very large literature on this subject. See, for example, the works of Marc Bloch and Albert Soboul for discussions of French rural society in the eighteenth and nineteenth centuries.)

Professor Fernand Ouellet has explained how the rural population of Lower Canada was afflicted with an agricultural crisis in the 1830's which combined with a commercial depression to sharpen a situation which had been deteriorating for some time. The French-speaking population had been faced with higher rent payments to the seigneurs, and a growing population had regarded with antipathy the settlement of land by the new British immigrants.[4]

Ouellet's analysis shows how the nationalism of the French-speaking Canadians first emerged in the early nineteenth century in conjunction with the definition of the class interests of a professional bourgeoisie. Both liberalism and nationalism developed amongst the professional class as they defined their interests in opposition to those of the merchants and the British administrators. The professionals and French-speaking small merchants saw the St. Lawrence as an inland sea, surrounded by a rural population. The British administrators, and of course the newly arrived English-speaking merchants, saw the St. Lawrence as the channel of colonial trade, the link between the colony and the new imperial centre. The liberal and nationalist opposition of the French-speaking professional class was later extended to the rural community as agricultural difficulties and the growth of population produced a reaction to the new colonial situation. The liberalism of the professional class was, however, outweighed in the Parti Patriote, which channelled the new nationalism into opposition to the colonial government while supporting the seigneurial regime and the church.

The Act of Union confirmed the intention of Lord Durham's Report with regard to the subordination of the nationalism of French-speaking Canada. But the French-speaking Canadian nation did not disappear. The rival nationalisms of Canada East and Canada West continued in an uneasy alliance. Confederation was seen as a way out of the conflict, but it was a solution that placed heavy odds against the French-speaking Canadians.

The Riel rebellion re-opened the national divisions which had been temporarily glossed over by Confederation. It became apparent that there were different opinions as to the character of the new society that was being created. George Brown had spoken for many in Upper Canada when he expressed his view of western expansion: "We hope to see a new Upper Canada in the Northwest Territory – in its well regulated society and government, in its education, morality and religion" (quoted in R. Cook, *Canada and the French-Canadian Question,* p. 33). At the end of the Quebec Conference in 1864, Brown privately expressed his views about Canada even more succinctly when he wrote to his wife: "French Canadianism entirely extinguished" (*ibid.,* p. 175).

Cartier, however, had hoped that Manitoba would develop along the lines of Quebec, and he was joined in this hope by many who saw in western settlement a chance to offset the minority position within the Confederation of French-speaking Canadians. Cartier might have had hopes for the western expansion of French-speaking Canada, but practically his acceptance of Confederation meant the rejection of the tradition of Papineau and support for the commercial interests of English-speaking Montreal. The testing of the meaning of Confederation in the Manitoba, and later the Ontario, schools question showed that even with Laurier as prime minister the French-speaking Canadian nation was not recognized as equal. French Canadians were to be treated as any other minority group.[5]

In French-speaking Canada Laurier was opposed by Henri Bourassa, who had left Ottawa in 1907, frustrated by Laurier's government. Bourassa did not, however, come to the conclusion that the French-speaking Canadians should reject Confederation.[6] Bourassa continued to believe in "a nationalism that was Canadian first and foremost" (Laurendeau, p. 136). But he did not mean by that a fusion of French- and English-speaking Canadians which would have meant the subordination of the minority. Rather he hoped for the recognition of the peculiar binational nature of Canadian nationalism, and an acceptance of one nation by the other. This complex view was made more so by the continuation of Canada's links with Britain and the strength of the "Imperialist idea" at this time. Bourassa was an anti-imperialist, looking towards an "authentic" independence for Canada, yet he drew back from demanding formal independence for fear of the "American colossus." He explained his position in a speech in 1901:

> Ce que je voudrais, c'est qu'entre la vieille frégate anglaise qui menace de sombrer et le corsaire américain qui se prepare à recueillir ses épauves, nous manoevrions notre barque avec prudence et fermeté afin qu' elle ne se laisse pas englouter dans le gouffre de l'une ni entraîner dans le sillage de l'autre. Ne rompons pas la chaîne trop tôt, mais n'en rivons pas follement les anneaux.[7]

Bourassa had claimed that Canada was a bilingual country in all provinces, but he saw that French-speaking Canadians were "being made provincials against our will." In fact, many French-speaking Canadian nationalists had turned back into Quebec in the nineteenth century. Generally this nationalism was of a conservative variety, associated with Church and rural society, but it is a mistake to over-emphasize this aspect. Industrialization and urbanization slowly changed the nature of Quebec throughout the nineteenth century. The social changes of the present century, which brought a renewal of a progressive and secular nationalism, did not occur suddenly at the end of the Duplessis regime to produce the Quiet Revolution out of the blue.

In the 1840's Etienne Parent of L'Institut Canadien was lecturing on the history of economic thought and drawing the conclusion that the preservation of the French-speaking Canadian nationality must be sought by means of industrialization. The significance of this analysis was made clear as industrialization, controlled mainly by "English" capital, undermined the national identity that had been sought in rural society. In 1906 Errol Bouchette published his study *L'Indépendance économique du Canada français,* in which he called for the creation of co-operative enterprises and the use of the resources of the provincial government to offset the dominance of "outside" capital. Bouchette's views had an effect on Bourassa and La Ligue Nationaliste Canadienne. (As did the example of Adam Beck and Ontario Hydro. See Brown and Cook, pp. 133–38.)

In 1909 Oliver Asselin of La Ligue Nationaliste Canadienne was calling for railway nationalization and the public ownership of hydro-electric power and, in addition, for a social program of welfare measures, a labour code, and the control of monopolies. (See R. Cook, "Quebec: The Ideology of Survival.")

The nationalist aspirations of French-speaking Canadians increasingly became identified with Quebec, which was seen as a potential nation state, rather than as just a province in the Canadian Confederation. In the period of the "Quiet Revolution" of the 1960's it became clear that the French-speaking Canadian nationalists had become Québécois nationalists. The creation of Hydro-Québec symbolized a new sense of power, a determination to be both "maîtres chez nous" and to create a society that would be a better home. This nationalist ferment created a reaction. "Federalists" from Quebec argued that these national aspirations could be accommodated within Canada as the whole country became "bilingual and bicultural."[8]

The problem with the federalist response has been that it is not an accommodation of French-speaking Canadian nationalism but a denial of its legitimacy. This has been particularly clear in the thought of the present prime minister. Before entering the Liberal government Trudeau had published a series of attacks on the nationalism which had been gaining strength in the 1950's and 1960's. Sometimes he argued from the "left": "the working class will pay for nationalism"; French Canadians "do not really believe in democracy" since they have not had to fight for it, quoting Frantz Fanon on the dangers of the "nationalist bourgeoisie"; sometimes he appealed to "technological laws," economic and technical forces, and the claim that "chauvinism equals economic inefficiency." He quoted Toqueville who equated public opinion and social discipline with tyranny, and Lord Acton who thought that "nationalism does not aim either at liberty or prosperity." The result was a curious combination of right-wing liberalism and left-wing polemics. (See P.E. Trudeau, *Federalism and the French-Canadians*). What was significant, however, was that in his denial of nationalism, Trudeau opposed the tendency towards "special status" that had been emerging in Quebec's relationship with the rest of Canada. The result was that the policies of bilingualism and biculturalism were caught in a political crossfire. Had they been advanced as a demonstration of the fact that Canada was in fact a binational state they might, if they had been accepted by English-speaking Canadians, have been of some interest to Quebec as well as of considerable importance to the large numbers of French-speaking Canadians living outside of Quebec. As it was, they were seen in Quebec as anti-nationalist and in English-speaking Canada as an attempt to appease Quebec by favouring one minority at the expense of the other ethnic groups. The feeling of French-speaking Canadians, centred in Quebec, that they are a conquered people was totally denied.

The rejection of the Liberal government's policy was demonstrated by the growing strength of the "*indépendantiste*" Parti Québécois. Founded in 1968 under the leadership of René Lévesque, the man who had been associated with the formation of Hydro-Quèbec, it took a remarkable 23 per cent of the vote in 1970.

If the Québécois already felt like a conquered people they were reinforced in this view by the federal government's use of the War Measures Act in October 1970. The majority of Québécois were opposed to the methods of the group calling itself the Front de Libération du Québec (FLQ) but they were not convinced by the government's claim that the FLQ represented a revolutionary force. The arrests and detention without warrant or charge of hundreds of Quebec nationalists was a brutal show of force which "was no more the remedy for the crisis than the FLQ its cause" (Fernand Dumont, "A Letter to My English-Speaking Friends," in *The Vigil of Quebec,* p. xv).

Neither the Liberals' carrot nor the Liberals' stick changed the determination of the Québécois nationalists to change their social and political structures.

> What the new consciousness of the 1960's led us to challenge radically was not the idea of federation, which is in fact one of the great ideals of this century, but the caricature of it represented by the Canadian Confederation. Always, and more than ever during the past decade, we have had the conviction that we are a distinct people, and it is as a free people that we desire from now on to conclude our alliances, or if you prefer the word, our federations. (*Ibid.,* p. xv)

*Regionalism and Nationalism*

There has been considerable confusion over the significance of the new nationalism in Quebec because of the existence in Canada of strong regional cultures which are intertwined with the national cultures. Confederation was in fact a political unification of existing societies which were both linked by common experiences and separated by their history and by different types of economic links with Britain.

Economically the regions that were amalgamated by Confederation were the Maritimes, the Canadas, and the West. Each was linked to Britain in a different way and each area was undergoing its own form of development. The Maritime region was primarily a mercantile economy oriented towards trade in the Atlantic. Perhaps the most independent of the regions, it had reached a level of political and social development comparable to, some would say in advance of, the Canadas at the time of Confederation. The West is not generally regarded as having achieved any degree of development until the late nineteenth century. It was, however, a distinctive civilization before Confederation, linked to Britain through Hudson's Bay.[9] The effect of Confederation was to redefine the links of these three areas with Britain and to re-orient the Maritimes and the West to Central Canada through the National Policy. In the case of the Maritimes the re-orientation turned into a slow process of attrition as its economy was marginalized and it became a region of economic decline. In the West the process was dramatized by the Riel rebellion and the forcefully demonstrated determination of the Canadian government to exercise its control over the region. The West was opened up to large-scale immigration, and a new society was created within its territory.

The West, like the Maritimes, was politically integrated with Central Canada through the Conservative and Liberal parties. Yet these two parties were unable to maintain the total allegiance of western interests. When it became clear after 1896 that the Liberals would continue the National Policy, thus rejecting free trade and the easy money policies sought by western farmers, the way was clear for the rise of new parties which expressed sectional as well as social conflicts and which saw the federal government as a main target. Regional inequalities produced by the National Policy were the main cause of the emergence of the Progressive movement in the early twentieth century. The Farmers Platform of 1910 in effect called for a new national policy based on sweeping tariff reductions and a substantial degree of free trade between Canada, the United States, and Britain. (See W. L. Morton, *The Progressive Party in Canada,* p. 62, for example.)

Regionalism, because of the federal nature of Canada, could be represented through provincial governments and it has been reinforced by the fact that the social forces that have been dominant in this century have given rise to a prominent role for provincial activity. Provincial governments shape the policies that concern mineral resources and mining, urban development, and utilities such as hydro-electric power and roads. In addition much of the service sector, such as education and health and welfare, is directly run by the provincial governments.

Notwithstanding the persistence of regional conflict, the re-orientation of the regions brought about by Confederation and the National Policy has produced a nation of English-speaking Canadians. It has produced a nationality which embraces a variety of cultures, and which is thus unusual since it is based neither on "ethnic" cohesion nor on the sense of a shared revolutionary past. The conquest of French Canada in the eighteenth century made Canada "British." This was changed as the pattern of economic development, reinforced by the substantial non-British immigration of the late nineteenth and twentieth centuries, made it clear that, despite the political trappings of the Crown, the British aspect of the nation would not survive in its nationality.

There is a distinctive Canadian culture, but its existence is often obscured. The culture is made very complex, not only by the regional components, but also by the history of the people as a population of immigrants. While important parts of the Canadian culture have been formed by the collective experiences of Canadians in Canada, these experiences have been modified, or interpreted, by reference to the cultural values brought by immigrants from varying backgrounds and not always shared by other immigrants. A constant flow of new people means that the total culture is always being modified at a rate which is probably faster than would be the case for a more homogenous population.

If the persistence of regional inequalities and ethnic differences has created a confusion in the nationalism of English-speaking Canada, this confusion has been deepened by the fragmenting influence of external factors which have led many Canadians to suffer feelings of inferiority and lack of identity. One of the outstanding features of the history of English-speaking Canada is that the society has taken a large portion of its cultural values from the centre countries which have dominated Canada, first Britain and then the United States. As a result, Canadians have frequently defined and understood themselves with the aid of interpretive concepts drawn from the experiences of Britain and the United States. In this century this phenomenon has been powerfully reinforced by the decline of local cultures and the invasion of the mass culture of the United States. Film, radio, and televison have all directed Canadian thought into American channels.[10]

In addition to the U.S. presence in the media there is a very strong American influence in the universities and schools. This combination distorts the perceptions of Canada and undermines the cultural integrity of the country. The consequences are of importance in all areas of our national life because our ability to control our lives has been markedly reduced.

The strength of imported cultural perceptions is particularly noticeable in the social sciences and this has had a destructive effect on the ability of Canadians to develop a social theory that corresponds to the characteristics of Canadian society. The difficulties of establishing a viable economic base for Canadian society are magnified many times by the distortion introduced by viewing the problem from outside the country. Liberal economic theory, which was developed first in Britain, and which in our own time has been most forcefully promoted in the United States, is at variance with the Canadian experience because it insists on the primacy of the role of the market.

The classical theory of development from Adam Smith on assumed that the growth of the market, which would allow productivity increases through the division of labour, was the key to development. David Ricardo extended Smith's argument with the theory of comparative advantage, which was held to demonstrate the benefits of the extension of the market internationally by means of unrestricted foreign trade.[11]

Not all economists accepted these views and it was seen in many countries in the nineteenth and twentieth centuries that there was a connection between industrialization and national policies, which controlled market forces. By mid-twentieth century the need for new theories of economic growth was widely perceived. The late Ragnar Nurkse, in his 1959 Wicksell Lectures, *Patterns of Trade and Development,* underlined the importance of the distinction between dominant and dependent economies and in particular pointed to the asymmetrical pattern of world trade between countries at different levels of development (p. 18, e.g.). As he put it, "the ideas of symmetry, reciprocity, and mutual dependence which we associate with the traditional theory of international trade are of rather questionable relevance to trade relations between the centre and the periphery" (p. 187).

In fact, many years earlier, in 1934, Harold Innis had gone much further in his indictment of liberal economics when he commented that "the success of *laissez-faire* has been paid for by the exploited areas of which we are one" (quoted in R. Neill, p. 61). Innis suggested that the problem facing Canadian economists was to recognize that planned growth was inherent in the national situation, but that control was contradicted by a need for foreign capital. In such a position, he warned:

> A new country, especially Canada, cannot afford to rely on the theory borrowed from old industrialized countries but she must attack with all the skill and industry she can command the task of working out a theory adapted to the situation in which she is able to defend herself against exploitation, against the drawing off of her large resources and against violent fluctuations which are characteristic of exploitation without afterthought. (Neill, p. 65)

The warnings of distinguished economists and the obvious inapplicability of large areas of economic theory did not have a visible effect on the success of liberal doctrines. The majority of Canadian economists did not wish to concern themselves with the concept of dependency. It was not until a new nationalism appeared in English-speaking Canada that the relevance of Innis' warning was understood.

For a generation, from the 1930's to 1960's, it seemed as though the continentalist view of Canada was held by the majority of the population. The decline of British power, political and economic upheavals in Europe, and the Second World War, had led many Canadians to see advantages in a close identification with the United States. By the 1960's, however, it became clear that the assimilation of Canada by the United States was producing a reaction. The reaction was not always clearly articulated as it emerged in diverse places. The three main political parties remained locked within continentalist assumptions. In addition, the nationalist movement was less strong in the more influential levels of society than in the people as a whole. Yet the emergence of the Waffle Group in the NDP and the founding of the Committee for an Independent Canada showed that a new political nationalism had come into existence.

This nationalism, like the nationalism of the Québécois, was not welcomed in all quarters. It was clear that a sensitive nerve had been touched. Implicit in the appeal to English-speaking Canadians to seek to express their own values was the reminder that they were not already doing so. Frequently explicit in the appeal was the argument that Canada was in fact dominated by the United States. The argument was thought by some to be unfriendly to our neighbour. Those who held a continentalist view of Canada reacted with outright hostility. While the facts were not usually disputed, its opponents sought to discredit nationalism as illiberal. It was "a doctrine of the discontented," an "uncontrollable force that may be temporarily allied with reform but almost always ends up in partnership with a community's more conservative instincts," and "an ideology developed to replace a lost sense of belonging."[12]

Yet the significant aspect of this English-speaking-Canadian nationalism was the result of the deep-seated and long-held view that Canada is worth preserving against the inroads of Americanization. Professor Rotstein argues that it is best understood as a countermovement:

> It is a response to the strains in the social structure, a form of political mobilization responding to the threat of erosion or disintegration of the basic institutions of the society. ... Nationalism is the symptom of distress, not a cause. The root cause, seen from a political vantage point, is the draining away of power and the possibility of self-determination. When crucial decisions are made outside the nation-state, nationalism represents the effort to restore this decision-making power and to safeguard the enduring institutions of a society. (*The Precarious Homestead*, p. 21)

The weakness of the response in English-speaking Canada was that, unlike Québécois nationalism, it was unable to articulate its position through a political party with a wide degree of support.

The decentralizing forces of regional inequality and continentalism remained stronger than the new nationalism. This was to have far-reaching consequences because it left only one aim for "national unity" – and that was pointed against Quebec nationalism. A broader and more fully understood English-Canadian nationalism, aiming at an end to Canada's dependency and its manifold consequences, might have provided the basis for a mutual reinforcement of the two Canadian nations. It might have provided the basis for an alternative national policy.

*Conclusion*

This century has seen the emergence of new social forces that have rejected some of the assumptions of the nineteenth-century liberal policies. The demand for more democratic forms of government through the extension of the franchise brought a demand for more social equality through the provision of social services. In addition there was a demand for more equality as the trade union movement demanded legislation to control the power of property owners and also demanded a reduction of the power of employers by insisting on a right to collective bargaining.

For a generation it was widely believed that the balance between market forces and central control had been resolved. Yet this modification of liberal economic theory has created some theoretical problems for liberal theory in general. How was it now possible to explain the remaining inequalities in society and why should private property in principle be sacrosanct if capitalism was not in fact able to provide economic stability and progress without economic planning? In general liberalism has had to retreat from its claims of universal progress and has resorted to the pragmatic support of political manipulation aimed at adequate growth, a low rate of inflation, reasonably full employment and a tolerably "just" society. Pragmatism was in fact promoted to a virtue rather than a necessary compromise. It was not until the 1970's that it became clear that this pragmatic liberalism, accompanied by "Keynesian" economic policies, was not a permanent solution. The problem was, as usual, economic as very high levels of inflation were combined with high unemployment and a recession that created fears of a return to the instabilities of the past. The labour movement, relatively quiescent in the years after the strike wave of 1946/47, showed a new militancy in the late 1960's and in the early 1970's.

This is not to say that liberalism has become unimportant. It has been associated with fundamental principles of civil equality and civil rights and these principles have to be of concern to those proposing alternative societies. Yet the association of liberalism with market economics also remains strong, despite the modifications of the mid-twentieth century. This association has created problems in all countries and especially in dependent countries such as Canada.

There have always been in Canada liberals who saw the need for a strong role for the government in order to ensure economic development. Even Lord Durham was able to modify his radical liberalism as he confronted the Canadian reality. In Canada, he argued, the state must be concerned with development and thus with public works. Durham rationalized this departure from his normal principles by likening the situation to wartime. Canadian society was at "war with the wilderness."

Under the influence of the staple theory, many economic historians have stressed the role of the government in creating a viable capitalist economy in Canada.[13] Innis even held the view that government ownership of some essential Canadian activities "rests ultimately on the Pre-Cambrian shield" (Hardin, p. 77).

In the nineteenth century many Canadians followed the example of both the United States and Germany in seeing a connection between national policies and industrialization (see M. Bliss, *A Living Profit,* p. 108), and politicians frequently found reason to oppose *laissez faire* doctrines. Macdonald argued that "Free Trade after the fashion of Jeremy Bentham, John Stuart Mill and John Bright" could not be "the bible, the catechism, the creed, and the paternoster of the political belief of Canada."[14] Sir Clifford Sifton argued that, though he had been raised on free-trade principles, "doctrines do not always apply to facts."

A Canadian "public enterprise tradition" was created in the face of American continental expansion. Canals, railways, and an airline network were developed with government ownership and extensive government support of private ownership because the development of all Canadian transportation systems was essential for Canadian development but could not be provided by the market economy. Market forces always provided continentalist alternatives. Conservative governments in Ottawa and the Provinces promoted government-owned utilities in order to offset the continentalist form of development under private ownership. Ontario Hydro and the Manitoba and Saskatchewan telephone systems are examples. A Canadian radio and television network was created as the result of the Canadian Radio Broadcasting Act, introduced by R.B. Bennett's government in 1932. As Graham Spry, the promoter of the Canadian Radio League, explained, it was once again a question of "the State or the United States."[15]

But as the liberal ideology, in its American version, has become dominant in Canada an important aspect of the Canadian identity has been obliterated. The growth of American corporations and U.S. government influence in Canada has meant the displacement of the Canadian public enterprise culture.

In the United States intervention in the market place is generally regarded as legitimate only in time of war or for the purpose of ending gross abuses. This position has been influential also in Canada where it creates an additional problem, for while the operation of market forces has limited the possibilities for democracy in all countries, in peripheral countries it has the additional effect of creating the problem of foreign economic control. This control both reduces the effectiveness of democratic control by citizens and jeopardizes the possibilities of economic development. In other words, the association of liberalism with market economics has created a barrier to both personal equality and national survival.

The St. Lawrence merchants did have a vision of economic development. But for them the river remained an axis of imperial trade, and ultimately their policy was rendered impotent in the face of the economics of empire. The politicians and men of property who supported the amalgamation of the colonies were able to believe that prosperity would ensue for all and that all regions of the new nation would develop in a complementary fashion. Economic development would pivot on the financial interests of Montreal and the railway companies but the federal government would assure a genuine national development. They did not by any means assume that equality of condition would be the result, but there was an expansive optimism about the future.

Yet a harmonious, integrated economic growth has not been achieved. The financial sector, and the service sector generally, have been overextended. There is a continued reliance on primary exports to promote prosperity, and the economy is largely under foreign control.

The national policy of the nineteenth century was unable to cope with the forces arrayed against it. It became the victim of the decisive collapse in the first half of the twentieth century of the international system of trade with Britain at its centre. It succumbed to the growth of U.S. corporations whose tentacles reached deep into Canada to tap its resources. But it was also defeated by its inability to deal with the divisive internal factors in Canadian society. In fact the old national policy perpetuated those internal divisions. Thus the task of Canadian politics remains that of devising a national policy that would allow Canadians to assume ownership of their own country. At the same time the policy would have to recognize the binational nature of Canada, redress regional inequalities, and provide for an extension of democratic control of Canadian society.

## Notes

**1.** Underhill saw Canada First as really "Ontario First." He also suggested that the time of Confederation marked the end of the period of liberal nationalism and the beginning of the "Bismarckian era." Professor Craig Brown also suggests that there was a change in Canadian nationalism at the end of the nineteenth century, as the Boer War injected a new sense of imperialism through the connection with Britain. (See Brown, "The Nationalism of the National Policy.")

**2.** See Alfred Dubuc, "The Decline of Confederation and the New Nationalism," in P. Russell, ed., *Nationalism in Canada*, pp. 112–32. Dubuc's article is particularly important because he recognizes that nationalism is not an homogeneous phenomenon, but varies according to the social circumstances that bring it into being. See also, for a view of nationalism as historically variable, E.J. Hobsbawm, "Some Reflections on Nationalism." For interpretations of Confederation in Quebec, see Ramsay Cook, *The Maple Leaf Forever*, pp. 68-81.

**3.** D.G. Creighton, "The Struggle for Financial Control in Lower Canada, 1818-31," reprinted in *Canadian Historical Readings*, no. 5, p. 34. Creighton characterized the social attitudes of the French-speaking Canadians as "unambitious, parsimonious," and governed by "primitive shrewdness and native parsimony." See also by Creighton, "The Economic Background of the Rebellions of 1837," reprinted in Easterbrook and Watkins, pp. 222-36.

**4.** See F. Ouellet, *Histoire économique et sociale du Québec, 1760–1850*, and also F. Ouellet, "Le Nationalisme canadien-français: de ses origines à l'insurrection de 1837," in *Canadian Historical Readings*, no. 5. Ouellet's argument is summarized in English in the text by P. Cornell, J. Hamelin, F. Ouellet, and M. Trudel, *Canada: Unity in Diversity*, pp. 174–81 and 216–28, and also in F. Ouellet, *Louis-Joseph Papineau: A Divided Soul*. See also Ouellet, "Les Insurrections de 1837–38: un phénomène social," *Histoire social/Social History*, 1968. Ouellet points out that a prolonged political crisis is likely to reflect the transfer of political and economic power between classes or ethnic groups, or both at the same time. He argues that French-speaking Canadian nationalism did not emerge at the beginnings of settlement because of the "pre-political" nature of the early society. Even the conflicts between 1760 and 1791 did not have a national character, although the Loyalist immigration created the basis for a future nationalism.

The rural opposition to the government in the 1830's is shown both by the increasing number of *charivaris*, aimed at the removal of militia officers and other government officials, and by the large numbers involved in the actual uprisings in 1837 and 1838. The rebels were mostly Canadiens, with a small number of Irish and Americans, and the leadership was supplied by farmers and artisans with support from day-labourers and younger men. There were elements corresponding to "primitive" rebellions in other countries as some rural people regarded Papineau as a "messiah." Ouellet argues that Papineau's leadership was indecisive because of the clash within himself, of the *patriot* and liberal.

**5.** In 1890 the Manitoba government ended the use of French as an official language in the province and abolished the separate school system. In 1912-13 Ontario passed legislation that had the effect of limiting the use of French in Ontario schools. Both Manitoba and Ontario used the legislation on provincial rights in education against pressure from the federal government to modify their positions.

**6.** On Bourassa, see the essay by André Laurendeau, in R.L. McDougall, ed., *Our Living Tradition*, 4th. Series. This is an English-language version of an earlier essay by Laurendeau, "Le Nationalisme de Bourassa," in the collection of essays *La Pensée de Henri Bourassa*. For a contrast with Bourassa, see J.W. Dafoe, *Laurier: A Study in Canadian Politics*. Dafoe was a firm believer in the single-nation view of Canada, with French-speaking Canadians relegated to a minority role.

**7.** Quoted in Laurendeau, p. 141. ("What I would like is that, between the old English frigate which threatens to founder and the American privateer which is getting ready to pick up the debris, we steer our boat with care and steadiness so that it does not become engulfed in the vortex of the one nor drawn into the wake of the other. Let us not break the chain too soon, but let us not foolishly strengthen the links.") Bourassa's position was complicated even further, especially in his later years, by his allegiance to the Roman Catholic Church.

**8.** On interpretations of federalism, see A.R.M. Lower et al., *Evolving Canadian Federalism;* and P.A. Crépeau and C.B. Macpherson, eds., *The Future of Canadian Federalism/ L'Avenir du féderalisme canadien*; Ramsay Cook has edited a collection of documents entitled *French-Canadian Nationalism.* Some useful studies of Quebec since World War II are: Parti Pris, *Les Québécois*; Marcel Rioux, *Quebec in Question*; P.E. Trudeau, ed., *The Asbestos Strike*; D. Drache, ed., *Quebec - Only the Beginning*; and Fernand Dumont, *The Vigil of Quebec.*

**9.** Professor Morton has made the point that the West was not simply the result of the imperialist expansion of Central Canada. See the essay by Carl Berger, "William Morton: The Delicate Balance of Region and Nation," in C. Berger and R. Cook, eds., *The West and the Nation*, pp. 9-32.

**10.** This subject has been discussed widely. See, for example, F.W. Peers, *The Politics of Canadian Broadcasting, 1920-51*, and H. Hardin, *A Nation Unaware*, Part 4. A recent contribution is S.M. Crean, *Who's Afraid of Canadian Culture*? A weakness of Crean's analysis is that she does not always distinguish between the social context of the presentation of "art" and its inherent artistic content. For example, the fact that in Canada opera is to a considerable extent supported by people who are concerned to demonstrate a certain social role by attending operas does not reflect on the artistic value of the opera itself. The fact that Beethoven's music or Shakespeare's plays are not well known to certain people does not mean that these artists have nothing to say to those people. (Neither of course does it mean that those people have no culture, though it does mean that they have missed something.) This is an important point in deciding what artistic values are to be supported to enhance a distinctively Canadian culture.

On the situation in the universities see R. Mathews and J. Steele, *The Struggle for Canadian Universities*. The Association of Universities and Colleges of Canada has added to the debate with the Report by T.H.B. Symons, *To Know Ourselves; The Report of the*

*Commission on Canadian Studies.*

**11.** The "theory of comparative advantage" was first explained by Ricardo using the examples of Britain and Portugal and the trade in cloth and wine. The irony of choosing England and Portugal is apparently still hidden to many economists who repeat the example in their textbooks and lectures.

A century before Ricardo's example, in 1703, England had signed the Methuen Treaty with Portugal which reduced English duties on wine from Portugal and Portuguese duties on cloth from England. The results were far-reaching. Portugal could not export sufficient wine to pay for the textiles. But Portugal had a colony, Brazil, which could supply the deficit with gold. The result was that Portugal was virtually bypassed, Brazil developed a large slave population to work the gold mines, and London became the banking centre of the world.

As a Portuguese minister, the Marquis de Pombal, observed, Portugal had been reduced to a state of dependency within the rapidly growing British economic system. (Furtado, *The Economic Growth of Brazil*, p. 38.)

**12.** These phrases are taken from R. Cook, *The Maple Leaf Forever*, pp. 199, 87, and 86. Professor Cook was one of the most prominent historians to confront Canadian nationalism. As he notes in his essay on "Nationalism and Nation-State" (in *The Maple Leaf Forever*), "nationalism as an ideology ... along with socialism, has been central to all political discussion since the French Revolution." We should of course add liberalism to the list of central ideologies, since socialism implies a debate with liberalism and the interaction of the two has been of critical importance in the development of liberalism. (See E.J. Hobsbawm, *The Age of Revolution*.) As is apparent from earlier chapters, I take conservatism to be merely a variant of liberalism. There are of course non-liberal political philosophies of the "radical right" which have been of major significance in some countries, but not in Canada.

Cook distinguishes between the "nation-state" and the "nationalist-state." The nationalist-state, he argues (p. 5) is "one in which the ideological demands of one cultural group or nation are forced upon all other groups within its borders." On the other hand the nation-state "is a political and juridical concept which seeks to protect the individual and collective rights of the inhabitants without reference to cultural or national ideological claims." The "nationalist-state" is a "garrison state," a nation-state is merely a state with fences. But it is hard to understand how, even within the terms of liberalism, one can talk of "individual and collective rights" without reference to cultural claims. Cook confuses the argument about nationalism by suggesting that a nationalist-state is one in which one nationality prevails over other nationalities in the same state. In particular, this suggestion is inadequate for the discussion of the problem which is created when one nation-state dominates another nation-state.

Cook argues (pp. 8-9) that a nation-state can exist without nationalism because the nation-state itself better "serves the practical purpose of organizing groups of people into manageable units and providing them with services which they need and which they can share: a railway, a medicare program, a publicly owned broadcasting system, an art gallery, an experimental farm, a manpower retraining program, a guarantee of equality for linguistic rights." What we do not need, he tells us, is large doses of nationalist rhetoric. We do not need a "moral equivalent of the CPR" but a "practical successor to it." Of course his last point is absolutely correct. The problem is how do you get a "practical successor to the CPR" in the present state of the Canadian economy? To argue that this can be done without reference to nationalist cultural values is to ignore the historical forces which have led to the creation of transcontinental railways, public broadcasting, arrangements for linguistic rights, and many other services which have been essential to Canada's survival.

**13.** See W.A. Mackintosh, *The Economic Background to Dominion-Provincial Relations* and also the articles by Buckley, Aitken and Fowke in W.T. Easterbrook and M. H. Watkins, *Approaches to Canadian Economic History.*

**14.** Quoted in C.D.W. Goodwin, *Canadian Economic Thought: The Political Economy of a Developing Nation, 1814–1914,* p. 56. Goodwin discusses the work of one of the few theoretical economists of the nineteenth century who did support tariffs, John Rae, a

Scot who settled in Upper Canada in the 1820's. In his *New Principles of Political Economy,* Rae argued that the priority of introduction of industry could itself be a basis for comparative advantage. In other words comparative costs were not fixed for all time.

**15.** See Hardin, part 4, "The Public Broadcasting Culture." Bennett gave as a reason for his government's decision the desire to foster national consciousness as well as creating a national communications network. Hardin explains the ideological importance of the CBC. It has allowed for the creation of a broadcasting culture that can reject the market-place culture of American broadcasting, which has become largely a vehicle for advertising and promotes a narrow individualistic consumerism.

# Bibliography

L'Action Nationale, *La pensée de Henri Bourassa,* Montreal, 1954.

I. Adams et al., *The Real Poverty Report,* Hurtig, 1971.

A. Aguilar, *Pan-Americanism; From Monroe to the Present,* Monthly Review, 1968.

H.G.J. Aitken, "The Changing Structure of the Canadian Economy," reprinted in J.J. Deutsch, B.S. Kierstead, K. Levitt, and R.M. Will, *The Canadian Economy: Selected Readings,* Macmillan, 1962, pp. 524-48.

———, "Defensive Expansion: The State and Economic Growth in Canada," reprinted in Easterbrook and Watkins, pp. 183-221.

R. Allen, *The Social Passion: Religion and Social Reform in Canada, 1914-1928,* University of Toronto Press, 1971.

B. Bailyn, *The Ideological Origins of the American Revolution,* Harvard University Press, 1967.

C.L. Barber, "Canadian Tariff Policy," *Canadian Journal of Economics and Political Science,* vol. 21, 1955, pp. 513-30.

R.J. Barnet and R.E. Müller, *Global Reach,* Simon and Schuster, 1974.

C. Berger, "The True North Strong and Free," in P. Russell, pp. 3-26.

———, *The Sense of Power: Studies in the Ideas of Canadian Imperialism, 1867-1914,* University of Toronto Press, 1970.

C. Berger, and R. Cook, eds., *The West and the Nation,* McClelland and Stewart, 1976.

G.W. Bertram, "Economic Growth in Canadian Industry, 1870-1914: The Staple Model and the Take-Off Hypothesis," reprinted in Easterbrook and Watkins, pp. 74-98.

M. Bliss, *A Living Profit: Studies in the Social History of Canadian Business, 1883-1911,* McClelland and Stewart, 1974.

T. Bottomore, *Classes in Modern Society,* Allen and Unwin, 1966.

———, *Marxist Sociology,* Macmillan, 1975.

P.L. Bourgault, *Innovation and the Structure of Canadian Industry,* Science Council of Canada (Special Study no. 23), 1972.

J.B. Brebner, *North Atlantic Triangle,* Carleton Library, 1966.
M.B. Brown, *The Economics of Imperialism,* Penguin, 1974.
R.C. Brown, *Canada's National Policy, 1883-1900: A Study in Canadian-American Relations,* Princeton University Press, 1964.
______, "The Nationalism of the National Policy," in P. Russell, pp. 155-63.
R.C. Brown and R. Cook, *Canada 1896-1921: A Nation Transformed,* McClelland and Stewart, 1974.
N. Bukharin, *Imperialism and World Economy,* Merlin Press, 1972.
W.L. Burn, *The Age of Equipoise,* Norton, 1965.
P. Burroughs, *The Canadian Crisis and British Colonial Policy, 1828-41,* Macmillan, 1972.

Canadian-American Committee, *A Time of Difficult Transitions: Canada-U.S. Relations, in 1976,* Montreal, 1976.
J.M.S. Careless, "Frontierism, Metropolitanism, and Canadian History," *Canadian Historical Review,* vol. 35, 1954, pp. 1-21.
______, "Metropolitanism and Nationalism," in P. Russell, pp. 271-83.
E.H. Carr, *International Relations Between the Two World Wars, 1919-1939,* Harper Torchbooks, 1966.
R.E. Caves and R. H. Holton, *The Canadian Economy,* Harvard University Press, 1961.
J.D. Chambers and G.E. Mingay, *The Agricultural Revolution, 1750-1880,* Batsford, 1966.
W. Clement, *The Canadian Corporate Elite,* McClelland and Stewart, 1975.
R. Cook, "Quebec: The Ideology of Survival," in Cook, *Canada and the French-Canadian Question,* Macmillan, 1966.
______, "La Survivance: English-Canadian Style," in Cook, *The Maple Leaf Forever,* Macmillan, 1971.
______, ed., *French-Canadian Nationalism,* Macmillan, 1969.
P. Cornell, J. Hamelin, F. Ouellet, and M. Trudel, *Canada: Unity in Diversity,* Holt-Reinhart, 1967.
S.M. Crean, *Who's Afraid of Canadian Culture?* General Publishing, 1976.
D.G. Creighton, *British North America at Confederation*, Queen's Printer, 1963.

———, *Canada's First Century,* Macmillan, 1970.

———, "Conservatism and National Unity," in R. Flenley, ed., *Essays in Canadian History,* Macmillan, 1939.

———, *Empire of the St. Lawrence,* Macmillan, 1956.

———, *Harold Adams Innis; Portrait of a Scholar,* University of Toronto Press, 1957.

———, "The Decline and Fall of the Empire of the St. Lawrence," and "Towards the Discovery of Canada," reprinted in Creighton, *Towards the Discovery of Canada,* Macmillan, 1972.

———, "The Economic Background of the Rebellions of 1837," reprinted in Easterbrook and Watkins, pp. 222-36.

———, "The Struggle for Financial Control in Lower Canada," reprinted in Canadian Historical Readings no. 5, *Constitutionalism and Nationalism in Lower Canada,* University of Toronto Press, 1969.

P.A. Crépeau and C. B. Macpherson, eds., *The Future of Canadian Federalism/L'avenir du féderalisme canadian,* University of Toronto Press, 1965.

M.S. Cross ed., *The Workingman in the Nineteenth Century,* Oxford, 1974.

R.D. Cuff and J.L. Granatstein, *Canadian-American Relations in Wartime,* Hakkert, 1975.

P.A. Cumming and N.H. Mickenberg, *Native Rights in Canada,* Indian-Eskimo Association of Canada, 1972.

J.W. Dafoe, *Laurier: A Study in Canadian Politics,* Carleton Library, 1963.

J.H. Dales, "The Cost of Protectionism with High International Mobility of Factors," and "Some Historical and Theoretical Comments on Canada's National Policies," reprinted in Dales, *The Protective Tariff in Canada's Development,* University of Toronto Press, 1966.

———, "Protection, Immigration and Canadian Nationalism," in P. Russell, pp. 164-67.

G. Dangerfield, *The Strange Death of Liberal England,* Capricorn, 1961.

R. Davis, *The Rise of the Atlantic Economies,* Weidenfeld and Nicolson, 1973.

J.G. Diefenbaker, *One Canada,* vol. 2, Macmillan, 1976.

G.W. Domhoff, *The Higher Circles,* Vintage, 1971.

D. Drache, ed., *Quebec — Only the Beginning,* New Press, 1972.

I.M. Drummond, *British Economic Policy and the Empire, 1919-39,* Allen, and Unwin, 1972.

F. Dumont, *The Vigil of Quebec* (trans. S. Fischman and R. Howard), University of Toronto Press, 1974.

A. Dunham, *Political Unrest in Upper Canada, 1815-1836,* Carleton Library, 1963.

J. Dunn, *Modern Revolutions,* Cambridge University Press, 1972.

W.T. Easterbrook and H.G.J. Aitken, *Canadian Economic History,* Macmillan, 1958.

W.T. Easterbrook and M. H. Watkins, eds., *Approaches to Canadian Economic History,* Carleton Library, 1967.

J. Eayrs, *In Defence of Canada,* vol. 3, University of Toronto Press, 1972.

Economic Council of Canada, *Fifth Annual Review: The Challenge of Growth and Change*, Queen's Printer, 1968.

——, *Looking Outward: A New Trade Strategy for Canada,* Information Canada, 1975.

J. Fayerweather, *Foreign Investment in Canada,* Oxford, 1973.

H.S. Ferns and B. Ostry, *The Age of Mackenzie King,* Lorimer, 1976.

D.F. Fleming, *The Cold War and Its Origins, 1917-1960,* 2 vols., Doubleday, 1961.

J. Fodor and A. O'Connell, "La Argentina y la economica atlantica en la primera mitad del siglo xx," *Desarolla Economica,* April-June, 1973.

V. Fowke, "The National Policy - Old and New," reprinted in Easterbrook and Watkins, pp. 237-58.

——, *The National Policy and the Wheat Economy,* University of Toronto Press, 1957.

A.G. Frank, *Capitalism and Underdevelopment in Latin America,* Monthly Review, 1969.

——, *The Sociology of Development and the Underdevelopment of Sociology,* Pluto Press, 1971.

R. Fumoleau, *As Long as this Land Shall Last,* McClelland and Stewart, 1974.

C. Furtado, *Development and Underdevelopment,* University of California Press, 1967.

———, *The Economic Development of Latin America,* Cambridge University Press, 1970.

———, *The Economic Growth of Brazil,* University of California Press, 1971.

J. Gallagher and R. Robinson, "The Imperialism of Free Trade," *Economic History Review,* vol. 6, 1953, pp. 1-15.

R.N. Gardner, *Sterling-Dollar Diplomacy,* Oxford, 1956.

P. Gay, *The Enlightenment,* 2 vols., A. A. Knopf, 1966, 1969.

E. Genovese, *The Political Economy of Slavery,* Vintage, 1967.

———, *The World the Slaveholders Made,* Vintage, 1971.

———, "Marxian Interpretations of the Slave South," in B.J. Bernstein ed., *Towards a New Past,* Vintage, 1969, pp. 90-125.

A. Giddens, *The Class Structure of the Advanced Societies,* Hutchinson, 1973.

W.I. Gillespie, "On the Redistribution of Income in Canada," *Canadian Tax Journal,* July-August 1976, pp. 419-50.

G.P. de T. Glazebrook, *A History of Transportation in Canada,* 2 vols. Carleton Library, 1964.

C.D.W. Goodwin, *Canadian Economic Thought: The Political Economy of a Developing Nation, 1814-1914,* Duke University Press, 1961.

W.L. Gordon, *A Choice for Canada,* McClelland and Stewart, 1966.

———, *Storm Signals,* McClelland and Stewart, 1975.

R. Graham, "Some Political Ideas of Arthur Meighen," in M. Hamelin, pp. 107-20.

J.L. Granatstein, *Canada's War: The Politics of the Mackenzie King Government, 1939-1945,* Oxford 1975.

G. Grant, *Lament for a Nation: The Defeat of Canadian Nationalism,* Carleton Library, 1970.

"Gray Report," *Domestic Control of the National Economic Environment: The Problems of Foreign Ownership and Control,* New Press, 1971.

E. Halévy, *The World Crisis of 1914-18,* Oxford, 1930.

———, *The Growth of Philosophic Radicalism,* Faber and Faber, 1934.

M. Hamelin, ed., *The Political Ideas of the Prime Ministers of Canada,* University of Ottawa, 1969.

H. Hardin, *A Nation Unaware; The Canadian Economic Culture,* J.J. Douglas, 1974.

R. Harrod, *The Dollar,* Macmillan, 1953.

L. Hartz, *The Liberal Tradition in America,* Harvest, 1955.

———, ed., *The Founding of New Societies,* Harcourt Brace and World, 1964.

C. Hill, *The World Turned Upside Down,* Viking, 1973.

E.J. Hobsbawm, *The Age of Revolution,* Mentor, 1964.

———, *The Age of Capital, 1848-1875,* Weidenfeld and Nicolson, 1975.

———, *Industry and Empire,* Weidenfeld and Nicolson, 1968.

———, "From Social History to the History of Society," *Daedalus,* Winter 1971, pp. 20-45.

———, "Some Reflections on Nationalism," in T.J. Nossiter, A.H. Hanson, and S. Rokkan eds., *Imagination and Precision in the Social Sciences,* Faber, 1972.

G. Horowitz, "Tories, Socialists and the Demise of Canada," *Canadian Dimension,* vol. 2, 1965.

———, "Conservatism, Liberalism, and Socialism in Canada: An Interpretation," *Canadian Journal of Economics and Political Science,* vol. 32, 1966, pp. 143-71.

M. Howard, *The Continental Commitment,* Penguin, 1974.

S. Hymer, "Partners in Development," *Newstate-ments,* vol. 1, 1971, pp. 4-14.

———, *The International Operations of National Firms,* MIT Press, 1976.

H.A. Innis, *Essays in Canadian Economic History*, University of Toronto Press, 1956.

———, *The Fur Trade in Canada*, University of Toronto Press, 1962.

———, *A History of the Canadian Pacific Railway*, University of Toronto Press, 1971.

———, "Great Britain, the United States and Canada," in Innis, *Changing Concepts of Time*, University of Toronto Press, 1952.

P. Jalée, *The Pillage of the Third World*, Monthly Review, 1968.

S. Jamieson, *Times of Trouble: Labour Unrest and Industrial Conflict in Canada, 1900-1966*, Privy Council Office, Task Force on Labour Relations Study no. 22, Queen's Printer, 1968.

L.H. Jenks, *The Migration of British Capital to 1875*, Nelson, 1963.

G.S. Jones, "The History of U.S. Imperialism," reprinted in R. Blackburn, ed., *Ideology in Social Science*, Fontana, 1972.

R.L. Jones, "French-Canadian Agriculture in the St. Lawrence Valley, 1815-1850," reprinted in Easterbrook and Watkins, pp. 110-26.

———, *History of Agriculture in Ontario, 1663-1880*, University of Toronto Press, 1946.

C. Julien, *America's Empire*, Vintage, 1973.

G. Kealey, ed., *Canada Investigates Industrialism; The Royal Commission on the Relations of Labour and Capital, 1889*, University of Toronto Press, 1973.

J.M. Keynes, *Essasy in Persuasion*, Norton, 1963.

———, *The General Theory of Employment, Interest, and Money*, Macmillan, 1961.

———, *Means to Prosperity*, in *Collected Writings of John Maynard Keynes*, vol. 13, Macmillan, 1972, pp. 335-66.

E. Kierans, *Report on Natural Resources Policy in Manitoba*, Government of Manitoba, 1973.

V.G. Kiernan, "Imperialism, American and European," reprinted in Kiernan, *Marxism and Imperialism*, Edward Arnold, 1974.

W. Kilbourn, ed., *Canada: A Guide to the Peaceable Kingdom*, Macmillan, 1970.

W.L.M. King, *Industry and Humanity* (ed. D. J. Bercuson), University of Toronto Press, 1973.

L. Knowles, *Economic Development of the Overseas Empire*, vol. 1, Routledge and Kegan Paul, 1928.

G. Kolko, *The Politics of War*, Random House, 1968.

———, *The Roots of American Foreign Policy*, Beacon, 1969.

G. Kolko and J. Kolko, *The Limits of Power; the World and United States Foreign Policy, 1945-54*, Harper and Row, 1972.

S. Langdon, "The Emergence of the Canadian Working-Class

Movement, 1845-75," *Journal of Canadian Studies*, vol. 8, 1973.

W. LaFeber, *The New Empire; An Interpretation of American Expansion, 1860-1898*, Cornell University Press, 1963.

W. Laurier, *Discours à l'étranger et au Canada*, Librairie Beauchemin, 1909.

J. Laxer, "The Political Economy of Canada" and "Manufacturing in the Canadian Economy," in R.M. Laxer, ed. *(Canada) Ltd.*, McClelland and Stewart, 1973.

R.M. Laxer, *Canada's Unions*, Lorimer, 1976.

V.I. Lenin, *Imperialism: The Highest Stage of Capitalism*, Progress Publishers, 1966.

K. Levitt, *Silent Surrender*, Macmillan, 1970.

G. Lichtheim, *Marxism*, Routledge, 1964.

______, *The New Europe*, Praeger, 1963.

______, *The Origins of Socialism*, Weidenfeld and Nicolson, 1969.

S.M. Lipset, *The First New Nation*, Basic Books, 1963.

A.R.M. Lower et al., *Evolving Canadian Federalism*, Duke University Press and Cambridge University Press, 1958.

N. McClung, *In Times Like These*, University of Toronto Press, 1972.

O.J. McDiarmid, *Commerical Policy in the Canadian Economy*, Harvard University Press, 1946.

R.L. McDougall, ed., *Our Living Tradition* (4th Series), University of Toronto Press, 1962.

G.F. McGuigan, "Administration of Land Policy and the Growth of Corporate Economic Organization in Lower Canada, 1791-1809," reprinted in Easterbrook and Watkins, pp. 99-109.

R.A. MacKay, *Canadian Foreign Policy, 1945-1954*, Carleton Library, 1970.

T.B. Macaulay, *The History of England from the Accession of James II*, vol. 1, Dent, 1964.

W.A. Mackintosh *The Economic Background of Dominion-Provincial Relations*, Carleton Library, 1964.

C.B. MacPherson, *The Political Theory of Possessive Individualsim*, Oxford, 1962.

______, *Democratic Theory: Essays in Retrieval*, Oxford, 1973.

H. Magdoff, *The Age of Imperialism; The Economics of U.S. Foreign Policy*, Monthly Review, 1969.

E. Mandel, *Europe vs. America; Contradictions of Imperialism*, Monthly Review, 1972.

H. Marshall, F.A. Southard, and K.W. Taylor, *Canadian-American Industry*, Carleton Library, 1976.

C. Martin, *"Dominion Lands" Policy*, Carleton Library, 1973.

D.C. Masters, *The Winnipeg General Strike*, University of Toronto Press, 1950.

R. Mathews and J. Steele, *The Struggle for Canadian Universities*, New Press, 1969.

R. Miliband, *The State in Capitalist Society*, Weidenfeld and Nicolson, 1969.

J.S. Mill, *Collected Works*, vol. 5, University of Toronto Press, 1967.

D.E. Moggridge, *Keynes*, Fontana, 1975.

W.L. Morton, *The Progressive Party in Canada*, University of Toronto Press, 1950.

R.T. Naylor, "The Rise and Fall of the Third Commercial Empire of the St. Lawrence," in G. Teeple, ed., *Capitalism and the National Question*, University of Toronto Press, 1972.

———, *A History of Canadian Business, 1867-1914*, 2 vols., Lorimer, 1975.

R. Neill, *A New Theory of Value: The Canadian Economics of H.A. Innis*, University of Toronto Press, 1972.

H.V. Nelles, *The Politics of Development: Forests, Mines, and Hydro-Electric Power*, Macmillan, 1974.

P.C. Newman, *Renegade in Power*, McClelland and Stewart, 1963.

———, *The Distemper of Our Times*, McClelland and Stewart, 1968.

R. Nurkse, *Problems of Capital Formation in Underdeveloped Countries and Patterns of Trade and Development*, Oxford, 1967.

P.R. Odell, *Oil and World Power*, 2nd ed., Penguin, 1972.

F. Ouellet, *Histoire économique et sociale du Québec, 1760-1850*, Fides, 1966.

———, *Louis-Joseph Papineau: A. Divided Soul*, Canadian Historical Association Booklet no. 11, 1968.

R.R. Palmer, *The Age of the Democratic Revolution*, 2 vols., Princeton University Press, 1959, 1964.

J.H. Parry, *Trade and Dominion; European Overseas Empires in the Eighteenth Century*, Cardinal, 1974.

Parti Pris, *Les Québécois*, Montreal, 1971.

F.W. Peers, *The Politics of Canadian Broadcasting, 1920-51*, University of Toronto Press, 1969.

N. Penner, ed., *Winnipeg, 1919*, Lorimer, 1973.

H.C. Pentland, "The Lachine Strike of 1843," *Canadian Historical Review*, vol. 29, 1948.

———, "The Development of a Capitalistic Labour Market in Canada," *Canadian Journal of Economics and Political Science*, vol. 25, 1959.

J. Porter, *The Vertical Mosaic*, University of Toronto Press, 1965.

R. Radosh, *American Labor and United States Foreign Policy*, Vintage, 1970.

M. Rioux, *Quebec in Question*, Lorimer, 1971.

H.L. Robinson, "Who Pays for Foreign Investment," *Canadian Forum*, May 1973, pp. 8-13.

———, "The Downfall of the Dollar," *Socialist Register*, 1973, pp. 397-450.

A. Rotstein, *The Precarious Homestead*, New Press, 1973.

"Rowell-Sirois," *Report of the Royal Commission on Dominion-Provincial Relations*, Queen's Printer, 1954.

R. Rowthorn and S. Hymer, *International Big Business, 1957-1967*, Cambridge University Department of Applied Economics Occasional Paper, no. 24, 1971.

P. Russell, ed., *Nationalism in Canada*, McGraw-Hill Ryerson, 1966.

A. Sampson, *The Sovereign State of ITT*, Fawcett Crest, 1974.

S.B. Saul, *Studies in British Overseas Trade, 1870-1914*, Liverpool University Press, 1960.

R.S. Sayers, *Financial Policy, 1939-45*, HMSO, 1956.

J. Schumpeter, *Imperialism and Social Classes*, Meridian, 1955.

B. Semmell, *The Rise of Free Trade Imperialism*, Cambridge University Press, 1970

Senate Committee on Poverty, *Poverty in Canada*, Queen's Printer, 1971.

J.-J. Servan-Schreiber, *The American Challenge*, Penguin, 1969.

O.D. Skelton, *Socialism: A Critical Analysis*, Houghton Mifflin, 1911.

A. Smith, *The Wealth of Nations*, Modern Library, 1937.

L. Smith, "*Le Canadien* and the British Constitution, 1806-10," reprinted in Canadian Historical Readings, no. 5, *Constitutionalism and Nationalism in Lower Canada*, University of Toronto Press, 1969.

L. Stephen, *History of English Thought in the Eighteenth Century*, vol. 2, Harbinger, 1962.

O. Sunkel, "The Pattern of Latin American Dependence," in V.L. Urquidi and R. Thorp, eds., *Latin America in the International Economy*, International Economic Association, 1973.

T.H.B. Symons, *To Know Ourselves; The Report of the Commission on Canadian Studies*, Association of Universities and Colleges of Canada, 1975.

M. Tanzer, *The Political Economy of International Oil and the Underdeveloped Countries*, Beacon, 1969.

E.P. Thompson, *The Making of the English Working Class*, Penguin, 1968.

T. Traves, "The Story that Couldn't be Told," *Ontario Report*, September, 1976.

S.M. Trofimenkoff and A. Prentice, eds., *The Neglected Majority*, McClelland and Stewart, 1977.

P.E. Trudeau, *Federalism and the French-Canadians*, Macmillan, 1968.

———, ed., *The Asbestos Strike* (trans. J. Boake), Lorimer, 1974.

M. Trudel, *The Seigneurial Regime*, Canadian Historical Association Booklet no. 6, 1971.

G.N. Tucker, *The Canadian Commercial Revolution, 1845-51*, Carleton Library, 1964.

C. Tugendhat, *The Multinationals*, Penguin, 1973.

F.H. Underhill, "The Development of National Political Parties in Canada," reprinted in Underhill, *In Search of Canadian Liberalism*, Macmillan, 1960.

———, *The Image of Confederation*, CBC, 1964.

R. Vernon, *Sovereignty at Bay*, Penguin, 1973.
J. Viner, *Canada's Balance of International Indebtedness, 1900-13*, Harvard University Press, 1924.

P.B. Waite, "The Political Ideas of John A. Macdonald," in M. Hamelin, pp. 51-67.
M.H. Watkins, "A Staple Theory of Economic Growth," reprinted in Easterbrook and Watkins, pp. 49-73.
———, "Economic Development in Canada," in I. Wallerstein, ed., *World Inequality*, Black Rose Books, 1976.
"Watkins Report," *Foreign Ownership and the Structure of Canadian Industry* (Report of the Task Force on the Structure of Canadian Industry), Privy Council Office, 1968.
R. Wiebe, *The Temptations of Big Bear*, McClelland and Stewart, 1973.
W.A. Williams, *The Tragedy of American Diplomacy*, Delta, 1962.
———, *The Contours of American History*, Quadrangle, 1966.
———, "The American Century," "The Large Corporation and American Foreign Policy," and "The Legend of Isolation in the 1920's," in Williams, *History as a Way of Learning*, New Viewpoints, 1973.
Woodrow Wilson Foundation and National Planning Association, *The Political Economy of American Foreign Policy*, Washington, 1955.
E. Wolf, *Peasant Wars of the Twentieth Century*, Harper and Row, 1969.
S. Wolin, *Politics and Vision*, Little Brown, 1960.